Try and Avoid the Speed Bumps

Try and Avoid the Speed Bumps

Donna T Cavanagh

To Deb Martin Webster, Richard Spall and Dr. Nancy Berk
For their honest and patient advice and their always
generous encouragement.

Preface

Try and Avoid the Speed Bumps is the follow up book to *Life on the Off Ramp*, my first collection of essays. This book contains essays and stories written between 2009-2012 including several which have not previously been published.

Contents

The Parking Garage .... - 11 -
Mom and Dad Moving and Storage .... - 15 -
Avoiding Sharks .... - 17 -
My Life Before Dogs .... - 20 -
Getting Married in Vegas…Again .... - 23 -
Up, Up and Away .... - 26 -
Am I Truly Depressed or Watching too Much Lifetime Television? .. - 29 -
Defusing a Hot Tub Disaster .... - 33 -
What Pole Dancers Need to Succeed .... - 36 -
The Life of a Pampered Pet .... - 39 -
He Might Only Have Eyes for Me But Where Are His Ears? .... - 42 -
Trying to Get Men to Date .... - 45 -
Leaving the Pasties Behind .... - 48 -
Small Feet Won't Get Me Into the Army .... - 51 -
What is My Fantasy Job? .... - 55 -
Will Video Poker Make Me Rich? .... - 59 -
Food, Hormones…and I Forget .... - 63 -
The Almost Demise of a Woodchuck .... - 65 -
The Devil Made Me Do It .... - 68 -
The Collateral Damage of a Friend's Breakup .... - 72 -
Can the Navy Seals Train my Dog? .... - 76 -
How to Avoid Guests and Other Paranormal Fun .... - 78 -
Stressed Out? Not When I Have my Hedge Clippers .... - 81 -
A Day in the Life of a Chocolate Frosting Addict .... - 84 -
Computer eHarmony? .... - 87 -
Mob Wives: Not Ladies One Invites to Tea .... - 91 -
In Search of a New Personality .... - 94 -
The Magic Shopping Machine .... - 97 -
Should I Star in a Workout Video .... - 101 -
The Speeding Ticket Gender Gap .... - 104 -
Learning to Read my Pets' Minds .... - 108 -
Hot Wax and Hurt Feelings Do Not Mix .... - 112 -
My Take on Social Media .... - 116 -
The Ultimate Proposal .... - 120 -
Tips on Do-It-Yourself Funerals .... - 123 -
Driving my Husband .... - 127 -
The Hot Tub Oasis .... - 131 -
The Fortune Cookie .... - 135 -
A Parent's Guide to Body Art .... - 139 -
The Literary Elite at Starbucks .... - 144 -
Every Dog Deserves a Ball…or Two .... - 147 -
Snuggie vs. Forever Lazy in the Battle to Stay Warm .... - 151 -

Flustered Over Flushing ....- 154 -
My Refrigerator and the Parallel Universe.....................- 157 -
Wedding Dreams and Nightmares ....- 160 -
The Deli Wars...- 164 -
They Don't Make Car Breakdowns Like They Used To ....- 168 -
Fur Flies at the Sonic Drive-In....................................- 171 -
Why Must There Always Be a Big Tease? ....- 174 -
The Umpire's Wife Has Been Ejected ....- 177 -
The Near Electrocution of the Cable Guy.....................- 180 -
My New Life as a Lawn Mower Racing Champion ....- 184 -
The Mom Dance..- 187 -
Is That Burning Hair I Smell? ....- 192 -
Old Friends and New Boobs ....- 196 -
The Psychic and the Internet Minister ....- 199 -
The Cleaning Lady Diaries ....- 203 -

The Parking Garage

"Try and avoid the speed bumps. I mean try *TO* avoid the speed bumps...not *AND*...*AND* is wrong," I told my daughter as she entered a parking garage in Philly.

"Mom, are we going to have a grammar lesson or a driving lesson? The speed bumps are in the middle of the road. It doesn't matter if it's *TO* or *AND*. Either way, I have to go *OVER* them."

I just shrugged my shoulders and let her do her driving thing. This excursion to downtown Philly was our fifth in our weekly outings we dubbed "the Learning Permit Marathon". The marathon was my husband's idea, and it began soon after my daughter got her permit. Let me correct that. It began immediately after she passed her permit test. My husband took her from the DMV to the Pennsylvania Turnpike and told her, "Drive." Some people thought we were crazy, and expressed their belief that new drivers should be transitioned to highways, but not my husband. In his defense, the professional driving school we hired concurred with his trial-by-fire instruction, and encouraged us to continue in between their lessons.

In weeks 1 through 4, I made her drive to various malls around the Philly area. I purposely picked malls that were not on our main stomping ground. The reward for the highway drives was lunch out or a new outfit. By week 8, she was comfortable on any highway, and her closet never looked better. But this parking garage in the middle of Center City had her unnerved.

I had to admit I had never driven in one of these garages before either. There was no gradual ascending ramp. Instead, the garage had a vertical road that resembled a spiral staircase and to drive it was a dizzying experience. On this sojourn, we had my daughter's friend in the backseat and when he saw the twisted path to the upper levels he leaned over into the front and said in a mischievous tone,

"Cool! Look at all the black marks on the walls. That's where people smashed into them."

Not amused by his observation, my daughter responded, "I think I should turn around; I don't think I can steer all the way up this thing."

I knew she was panicked, but there was no turning around, and I emphasized this fact by pointing out that there was a stream of cars lined up behind us and we were stuck.

"I know this looks like a challenge, but either you start steering up this twisty thing or we are going to be killed by the impatient drivers waiting to get into this garage. Just take a deep breath, keep the wheel turned and go."

Surveying this spiral structure, I realized there was little room for error. So, my daughter inhaled and began her ascent. It went pretty smooth except that she refused to go over five MPH which ticked off the people behind us, and she screamed out loud the entire ascent up the twisted monster. I am not talking a little girly squeal. No, her screams were at such a high pitch that I worried that the cement walls might crumble in pain. I think the screams may have seemed louder than they truly were because Mr. Wonderful in the backseat had opened his windows so my daughter's hysteria would echo.

Finally, we got to the top level, and we saw light at the end of the tunnel. She sped onto the straight, flat pavement ahead and parked in the first open space. We jumped out of the car, and it might be my imagination, but I think I felt my poor baby (the car – not my daughter) emit a loud sigh of relief. We made our way into the garage elevator where we were joined by two men in business suits. When the doors closed, they started to laugh. We must have looked a bit perplexed because one of the men said,

"We are so sorry. We were behind you going up the ramp. I never saw or heard anything like that in my life. We could not stop laughing."

"She's a new driver; she has her permit..." I quickly explained. But before I could get another word out, he put up his hand and said,

"Quite alright. You made our day. But next year, when my daughter gets her permit, there is no way in hell I am taking her here." He then looked at my daughter and said, "You did really well on the steering by the way, but it was the sound effects that I will always remember."

My daughter was mortified; I was a bit embarrassed as well, and my daughter's friend had a good story to share which he gladly did to anyone who would listen. My daughter had to endure about a week of torturous ribbing at school, but then week 6 was upon us, and for this trip, we went nowhere near the city. No, I took her to the Amish Country where the most challenging obstacle she faced was a slow-moving buggy.

Mom and Dad Moving and Storage

My daughter and I stood waiting for my husband to back our rented cargo van into the loading space in the IKEA parking lot. On our store cart sat a box spring and mattress for a queen-size bed plus 18 cardboard boxes whose contents contained my daughter's yet-to-be assembled bedroom set which we were going to move into her new apartment. I'm not sure why my husband, daughter and I thought we could handle this move on our own, but it became quickly apparent we bit off more than we could chew. However, let me say in our defense that we were not naïve. We had four years of moving her into college apartments under our belt, but for this move, we needed Superman or at least two guys on a steroid overload.

After my husband backed up the van, I opened the rear doors. Already inside the van was a sofa that my brother had donated for my daughter's new digs. I looked at the full cart, and I looked inside the van, and I knew we were in trouble. The box spring was first to go into the truck and that was not bad. The problems started when we attempted to maneuver the mattress in next to it. We shoved the mattress half-way in, but it would go no further. In the front cab, my daughter and my husband pulled the mattress toward them. I pushed it from my location inside the van where I was sandwiched between the box spring and sofa with the mattress sort of lying on top of me. Since I was underneath the mattress, I was not aware that other IKEA shoppers had gathered to watch this performance.

"Push! Just a little more!" my husband yelled.

"I am pushing! I'm pushing as hard as I can," I groaned in a very loud voice.

"Just a little more – push! You can do it!"

I was surprised when a man leaned in the van, and even though he could not see me buried under the furniture, asked, "Do you need help? Should I call an ambulance?"

"No, I don't think we are that bad off. We're okay," I gasped.

After we got the mattress secured, I inched my way out of the van and was taken aback by the crowd that had formed. The man who had asked to help saw my puzzled look and said,

"We thought you were giving birth."

"Get outta here! Me? Hey, I might be able to push a mattress into this van, but I'm not pushing anything out in this van."

Disappointed that no new baby named IKEA had arrived on the scene, the crowd dispersed, and we moved on to our next phase of labor and delivery which was delivering the furniture to her apartment. Lesson learned: Next time she moves, we hire professionals or at least an athletic OB/GYN.

Avoiding Sharks

I had lunch with my high school friends last week, and we started to talk about exercising which led to my one friend talking about this triathlon event that is being held in her New Jersey shore town. She thought it might be fun if I participated in it. While I tend to jump at a good challenge, I begged off this one as this event had something that I could not do: a 300-yard swim in the ocean.

I know what you are saying, "Three hundred yards–no biggie." Well, it is a biggie when you have just been running or cycling before jumping in the water. But to be honest, it's not the physical stamina that scares me about the ocean swim: it's the sharks.

I know the chances of me being eaten by a shark on that very day are probably like three million to one. After all, there will be a lot of people in the water, and so a shark would literally have a smorgasbord of swimmers to appease his or her appetite. But I know he would choose me. Why? Because a shark would sense my deep fear.

It's not that I do not go in the ocean. I ride waves and frolic with the best of them, but the triathlon swim is beyond the surf and to train for it, I would have to swim by myself in the early morning hours when as we all know sharks like to eat. I know I should train with a buddy, but that wouldn't be fair to the buddy. At the first sight of a fin, I would hand my buddy over to the shark while I make a beeline back to shore. I have no delusions of bravery here.

I have tried to conquer my fear of sharks. I rent a shore house every year during the Discovery Channel's *Shark Week*. I do this to face my fear. I figure a week of watching people being devoured and chewed to shreds on TV will de-sensitize me to the whole shark thing and make it easier to go in the water. Have I ever had an occasion to meet a shark? Only at the aquarium, so I guess that really does not count. My entire fear stems from the fact that I imagine that as soon as I step into the waves, sharks out in the ocean depths are saying,

"Okay, she is in the water, let's get lunch."

This is why I never open my eyes under water in the ocean. I don't want to see the shark staring at me. I figure this is one of those times that it is best not to know what is coming at you. If I had to analyze my fear, I would guess it has always existed inside of me but exploded outward when the first *Jaws* movie came out. I was young and impressionable. Even then, I knew that if I was going to see this movie, I needed to see it where I would be safe. So, I flew to my uncle's house in Chicago and saw it there. Okay, he was flying me out anyway, but it was a good excuse to see the flick then, and I knew I had to see the movie because when I returned to school that fall everyone would be talking about it, and I didn't want to be the only one who did not watch the most popular movie of the summer. Apparently, my fear of grammar school peer rejection outranked my fear of sharks at that point in my life.

Has my fear of sharks affected any other areas of my life? Well, I can never move to Florida. First off, that state is the not only the shark capital of the world, but the alligator or crocodile capital as well. And here we have fear number two. I never had to think about alligators much growing up in the New York City area or now in the Philly area where I live, but again, thanks to the Discovery Channel and of course, the internet, I have viewed graphic pictures of alligator attacks. My biggest fear with the alligators is that I will fall into some river or swamp and never be found again, or worse, I will witness an alligator eating one of my dogs. I heard that happens a lot in Florida.

As I think about it, I am pretty grateful to live in the Philly area. Sure, we have really tough sports fans, but we don't have sharks or alligators and the safe haven of the Poconos is just a short car ride away, and there are no alligators or sharks up in the mountains...but there are Copperheads. Damn, I forgot about my fear of snakes.

My Life Before Dogs

I had to take my dog, Frankie, to the vet for a wellness check. Usually, I try to do this at night so that someone can be at home with my other dog, LuLu, who does not like to stay by herself in the house. She gets nervous, piddles and then hides. When I do arrive home, she does not greet me. Instead, she makes me play hide-and-seek, and to her credit, she never hides in the same place twice, so the game gets annoying quickly.

This time, I had to make the vet appointment for the morning because our evenings were filled with just normal everyday crap which left no time for anyone to be on vet duty with me. So, on the morning of the appointment, I decided to wait for everyone to head to work before I got the vet trip underway. When my daughter drove off, I sent LuLu out to the backyard, so she would not see me putting on Frankie's leash. A leash to LuLu means "We're going for a walk, YAY!!" and I hate giving her false hope. Once LuLu was being entertained by the birds , I quickly put on Frankie's leash and escorted her to the car. Then, I ran back into the house, brought in LuLu, who looked puzzled as to why she couldn't find Frankie, her best friend and main tormentor, and ran back to the car to head to the vet.

I figured it took LuLu about 20 minutes to realize Frankie was gone. At first, there was probably a bit of panic until she realized that no one was sniffing her butt, licking her ears, or stealing her toys. When she did comprehend that Frankie was not in the house, she most likely performed the

"Yes, I am free, and I can do what I want" dance. This dance pretty much entails the dog squirming on her back with her legs up in the air.

We got to the vet, and Frankie was prancing along without a care in the world until she saw the entrance to the building. This is where she put on the brakes and would not budge. I tried treats, commands--nothing. It's as if someone superglued her butt to the pavement. One of the vet techs saw me pulling on the dog and came out to see if she could help. I asked her to hold the door while I half-carried, half-dragged the 85-pound moose into the vet's waiting room.

The tech put us in a room right away because she didn't want Frankie "corrupting the mood of the other dogs" in the waiting room. In other words, my dog was a bad influence. In Frankie's defense, I do know why she gets like this at the vet. She has memories of being at this hospital when she was sick as a puppy. I think she has Post-traumatic Parvo Stress, and it manifests itself via a really bad attitude.

I tried to calm Frankie down while we were in solitary. Finally, the vet came in and said, "Frankie you are such a pretty girl; we don't need to muzzle you, do we?"

And I said, "Yes, muzzle her. I just had to carry the damn pooch through your doors and I don't think she is going to be thrilled when you shove that thermometer up her butt."

And he said, "Mom sounds like she is having a bad day?"

I inhaled deeply and shut my mouth because I knew I would meet this vet again when it was time for LuLu's wellness check in two weeks. Despite the prods and pokes, Frankie was a gentle trooper. So, I decided to be brave, and as it turns out, stupid and asked the vet if he could cut Frankie's nails. He said the techs would gladly do that for me. He left the room, and the vet techs took over. One said it would be best to lay Frankie on her side and hold her head down. I thought this was a bad idea, but they insisted. They held her down and after the first snip, Frankie went berserk and knocked everyone down. She jumped on me for protection and that nail that was now so sharp from being partly cut landed in my forearm, and didn't stop until it had sliced all the way down to my thumb.

After the blood spurted, the vet people apologized as they tried to stop the dog from bolting from the room. Woozy from blood loss, I had to sit. Luckily, the vet had people bandages too, and after they were sure that I had not severed an artery, they sent us on our merry way with a new toothbrush for Frankie and a $20 coupon for our next visit.

When we finally got home, LuLu was nowhere to be found and Frankie took off to hide in her crate. I didn't look for LuLu immediately. I sat down and examined my wounds and tried to remember my life before dogs.

Getting Married in Vegas...Again

Last year, for our wedding anniversary, I convinced my husband to plan a trip to Las Vegas so we could renew our vows in the Elvis Chapel. Had I suggested renewing our vows in a quiet backyard ceremony, he would have nixed the idea, but anytime you put Las Vegas into the picture, he is ready to go.

I had never been to Las Vegas, so I was anxious to see what all the fuss was about. Another extra bonus for this trip was that our daughter could come along too. She turned 21, so what better way to ring in her legal age than a trip to Sin City. I also thought it would be great if she could be my maid of honor at this ceremony.

When I made the reservations for the wedding chapel, the nice woman on the phone asked if I wanted the skinny Elvis or portly Elvis to perform the ceremony. I opted for the skinny one because I like the movies with the younger Elvis. He is handsome and not so sweaty looking. She booked the skinny Elvis and told me that they would take care of everything else. I did not have to plan a thing, and they were true to their word.

With the ceremony planned, I set out to find a dress. I got a great dress–a blue cocktail dress. When I described my dress to my friends, they gave me a disappointed, "You didn't get a white one?"

"Come on," I responded. "It was a stretch wearing a white dress the first time around, but I was younger and could pull it off. This time I went with a more honest color."

What I didn't tell my friends was that when I was shopping, I saw a red dress I liked a lot, but the saleswoman told me that a red dress, even for a renewal ceremony shouted "Tart". Yep, Tart was the exact word she used. Not wanting my Elvis ceremony to reflect a "tart" theme, I went with the blue.

The Elvis people sent a limo for us, and we marched through the hotel in our wedding finery. People kept shouting "Good luck!" I gave my best Queen Elizabeth wave back to the well wishers. Well, I forgot I was in heels. If there is one person in this world who should not attempt any physical movement while wearing heels, it is me. I lost my balance and literally fell into the back of the limo. Luckily, I was wearing underwear.

When we got to the chapel, the hostess escorted my husband to the front of the aisle, and my daughter and I to a backroom. Our Elvis minister came into the room to go over the ceremony. He had on the white jumpsuit opened to the navel and a colorful lei around his neck. He also appeared to be about 60. Hm. I didn't expect him to be this old, but I guess this is what Elvis would have looked like if he got off the drugs and lived another 20 years. Then Reverend Elvis burst into song and serenaded us with "Fools rush in".

He had a very nice voice, but my daughter lost it, and then I lost it. We share this giggle trait. When we are nervous, we giggle, and for some reason, we were both nervous. Skinny Elvis didn't seem to mind though, and he sent my shaking-with-laughter daughter down the aisle. Then he took my arm and as he crooned "Love Me Tender", he escorted me to the front of the chapel.

The chapel also did a live feed so our relatives and friends back on the east coast could tune in. I will be blunt: I do not video or photograph well. Ask my mother. She will tell you flat out that I do not take good pictures. My original wedding album contains about five pictures because we could not find any photos of me where my eyes stayed open. On video, my hair takes on a life of its own, and my voice makes Minnie Mouse sound like a baritone.

When it was all over, we took a lot of pictures with Elvis, and they gave us a DVD to have as a remembrance of this special day. We watched the DVD that night in the hotel, and I made a mental note to order a month supply of Nutrisystem as soon as I got home.

Now that I have thinned down again, I want to go back to Vegas and redo the ceremony in front of the camera. I am determined to look good. This time I won't go the Elvis route. I saw a place that does a vampire theme. It might take a lot of convincing to get my husband to participate in a blood-letting-themed renewal ceremony, but he might give in if I let him spend a day at Sportsbook. After all, marriage is about compromise, and nothing says romance like a chomp on the neck.

Up, Up and Away

I would like to discuss Erectile Dysfunction. Obviously, I do not suffer from the malady, and when I told my husband I was writing about this, he emitted a loud gasp and then insisted that I make it very clear that he does not suffer from the malady as well. You men are so protective over your "boys", and I think it's been this way since the dawn of time. Females are protective of their "womanhood" too, but honestly, until Georgia O'Keefe and her paintings came along, many of us were not even sure what was down there to protect.

I apologize as I am getting off topic. What I truly want to discuss is the advertising for Erectile Dysfunction or E.D. The most annoying commercials to me are the ones that show a middle-aged-to-almost-senior couple doing work around the house when suddenly the "love bug" hits the man. I guess the point is that the "love bug" can still hit the man because he takes this drug. As I have said many times before, I am all for sex, so if this drug helps the guy have a great love life, then it's worth the pharmaceutical co-pay.

The commercials start off nice enough. The couple cuddles and hold hands, and they both have that "come hither" look in their eyes. Then they take a romantic stroll into the woods, get naked and sit in separate bath tubs. Can someone explain to me the point of separate bath tubs? Is it a censorship thing like when Lucy and Ricky couldn't sleep in the same bed because people might assume they were having sex?

I would think if you are advertising a drug that enhances one's sex life, you want people to assume the man and the woman do things besides take a bath in different tubs. Why aren't they sitting in a big Jacuzzi bathtub or a backyard spa? I think the separate bath tubs are a little misleading. No one can have sex while sitting in separate tubs. I don't care how endowed the guy is.

Anyway, if you take the time as I did to go on You Tube and search out these commercials, you find some truly interesting ones from Viagra®. At least one of these ads has been banned. Are they funny? Absolutely. Are they off-color? For sure, that is why they are funny. But I don't think that is why the commercial was banned. I think the people who oversee ads (Is that the great and powerful FCC?) probably thought the drug promised much more than it could deliver. I will give you a hint: The man in the commercial is doing pushups with no arms.

I guess the problem with the Viagra commercial was that it was too up front (no pun intended). There is a commercial for a natural enhancement product that addresses the whole impotence problem with visual symbolism. There are pointy objects and hoses and a plethora of other symbols almost hidden from view. This commercial reminds me of the "Can you find?" puzzles that are in kids' books. You know, where you have to circle the objects that have to do with a certain theme? I guess the theme in this ad would be phallic symbols.

There is no lack of creativity with these commercials, and they are fun until they divulge the potential side effects of the drugs. It's nice that men can have sex again but at what cost? I know men are saying, "Hey, we have been subjected to feminine hygiene products for decades. It's our turn to have our needs met."

Men are right; fair is fair. The E.D. commercials are addressing a true medical disorder – a medical disorder that has been swept under the rug for years. Maybe these drugs are making relationships last longer. I have to say that I know a lot of people who walk around with smiles on their faces nowadays. Maybe they are high on life or high on something else.

Am I Truly Depressed or Watching too Much Lifetime Television?

Lifetime Television: the place to go when I want to fall into a deep depression or when my hormones are totally out of whack. I guess Lifetime won't hire me to come up with their marketing slogans, but this is how I feel. This channel is not satisfied until every last teardrop hiding in my body has burst through my eye sockets. And I'm not talking about a single glistening teardrop that rolls gently down my chubby cheek. No, I am talking hysterical, give-my-face-red-rashes-from-bawling-like-crazy tears.

I guess when it comes down to it, the waterworks are my fault. Since I work from home, my number one rule is that the TV does not go on until after 5 PM unless I want to play a little hooky and watch an old classic movie. Recently, I did play hooky and turned on the TV which happened to be on the Lifetime channel. I started to watch a movie that was already in progress, but still, I got engrossed in it, and it had one of my favorite Lifetime actors, Patty Duke.

Patty Duke is the quintessential mother in all the Lifetime flicks. For some reason, she always portrays the perfect, sweet, southern mom whose kid gets knocked off by a serial killer or deranged spouse. The ensuing grief inspires her to turn into Mother Detective so that her child's murderer can be brought to justice. And she does all this while taking care of an invalid mother, a philandering husband, and her infant grandchild, who is usually the offspring of the murder victim.

Get all that? Anyway, this Patty Duke movie had pretty much the same plot, and as I predicted, Patty caught the murderers and then gave this heart-wrenching speech which resulted in massive amounts of water erupting from my tear ducts. As I was convulsing in sobs, I was cursing myself for falling into the Lifetime trap. And while this movie was on, the promos for another film premiering kept playing, and the new movie contained the next most popular theme in Lifetime flicks: women in prison.

The upcoming flick was about Amanda Knox, a girl about my daughter's age, who was locked in an Italian prison for killing her roommate. My mother mind began to panic, and I came up with a game plan and a list of lawyers who can handle foreign criminal cases in case my daughter found herself in the same predicament. Logically, I know that my daughter works for a company that is just 15 miles from home, and she doesn't have to travel for business so her chances of foreign imprisonment are slim at best, but if it happens on Lifetime, it can happen in real life, so it's best to be prepared.

I have learned from the Lifetime channel that women wind up in prison for the most bizarre reasons. In another one of their films, which is also based on a real-life event, the female protagonist was hauled off to jail for something her husband did. Yes, he was supposedly involved in espionage and just because they were married, she was considered an accomplice. So, the FBI raided her house and took her away in handcuffs, and let me just say that her first night in prison was not a welcoming experience. So, once again my mind wandered, and I thought about how I would handle prison.

First problem, I don't look good in orange, and in fact, that color gives me migraines. I wonder if I could plead a disability and get a softer color jumpsuit to wear. Yes, this was a concern in my totally freaked out mind, so I put "different colored jumpsuit" on my to-do list of things to find out about right after finding lawyers who handle Americans in foreign prisons. My next week calendar was filling up quickly with research about stuff that will probably never happen but needed to be addressed if I was ever going to have a good night's sleep again.

After the prison movie was done (and by the way, the woman was exonerated and sent home to rebuild her shattered life which will forever include pictures of her with messed up hair on the internet because police photographers never give prisoners a chance to fix their "do" before they snap the mug shot), I marched upstairs to my bedroom and demanded to know exactly what my husband did for all those years he traveled overseas for business because I didn't want to get arrested if he was up to no good. After seeing that flick, I knew there was no way I was doing time for him. I would sing to the Feds the first chance I got.

Although he was half awake, he looked at me and mumbled,

"Are you watching Lifetime again? I thought we agreed NO MORE LIFETIME."

And with those words uttered, he fell soundly asleep and ignored me, so I added one more thing to my research list: divorce lawyers.

Defusing a Hot Tub Disaster

Many people are aware of the relationship I have with my hot tub or as those in the industry call it, my "spa". My spa came to me in 2005. I fell in love with a simple, five-seat model which fits perfectly into one corner of my covered porch. The salesman also introduced me to the "bells and whistles" model, but he knew it was not for me. I didn't need a retractable TV or a built-in stereo system; I just needed the jets and the promise of peace and quiet.

Okay, I did get one upgrade: the light bulb that makes the water change colors. Was it necessary? Well, if you talk to my Feng Shui friend, she will tell you it was absolutely necessary. The water color triggers the right response from my mind so that I can have the ultimate hot tub experience. Did I buy all that? Well, I bought it more because the upgraded light bulb was only an additional $100. If it had been a $1,000 upgrade, I would have kicked her Feng Shui ass out of my spa.

Anyway, we do maintenance on the spa just as the owner's manual says because my husband, the engineer, lives and dies by the words in owner's manuals. Every three months, we drain the tub, wipe it down, change the filter and fill it back up again. It's a simple routine, and one that my spa appreciates. Last month, my multi-colored light burnt out, and I have not had a chance to order a new one. I mention the burnt out bulb because I think not replacing it right away might have caused my hot tub to be mad at me.

We emptied the tub right on schedule. Everything went perfectly until I tried to turn the power back onto the spa. I pushed the breaker, and it tripped; I pulled it a second and third time, but it kept tripping. My husband shook his head but couldn't figure it out. We thought maybe something that should not have gotten wet got wet during the emptying process, so we decided to give it a few hours. But alas, nothing worked. The tub would not stay on.

If this had been my washing machine or any other appliance, I would have been annoyed. But my hot tub? I was panicked. And it was a Sunday, so there was no one to calm me down. I imagined that my hot tub was toast and I would never soak in it again. I would never have that sense of Nirvana that I have come to expect from soaking in those blissful waters. I was not a joy to be around.

Monday morning, at 9 AM on the dot, I called Pelican, the wonderful people who brought the hot tub into my life. Kathy in service came to my rescue. She diagnosed the problem right away, and set up a service appointment for that Wednesday and then she said,

"You know, I can tell you what to do to fix this yourself."

"Me? Really?"

So, Kathy told me what tools I needed and talked me through the repair. There was a technical name for the problem, but honestly, I was too flustered at first to hear what she was saying, but she calmed me down, and we began. I felt like I was on one of those cop shows where the bomb squad has to talk the poor schmuck, locked in the room with the bomb, through the deactivation process. I unscrewed the panel and located the right cylinder and the screw to that cylinder, and I then used my wrench to gently turn that screw. I felt the sweat beading up on my forehead, and then water from the cylinder started to drip out and then it flowed out and then I tightened the screws again and I turned on the breaker and the power stayed on. And they say there are no miracles!

I called my husband at work and, of course, got his voice mail, so after the tone, I yelled "I fixed it! The hot tub is back." I called my daughter at work, and she wasn't as nearly impressed with me as I was. I told my friends; I announced it on Facebook. I had my Nirvana back!

As it turned out, no one was nearly as impressed with my spa repair job as I was. They said, "So, it was just a few screws", but none of them knew how to fix it ahead of time. They tried to rain on my hot tub parade, but I would not allow them. No, as I sat in my spa that night appreciating those jets, I felt a sense of pride and accomplishment and I thought, "Hm. Maybe I am ready to finally take that auto repair course. How hard can it be?"

What Pole Dancers Need to Succeed

I was thinking about getting my husband new golf clubs, but a friend of mine mentioned that maybe all he needed were new grips for his clubs. I didn't really understand the concept of new grips. Why pay just as much for new tops for the clubs, if for the same price, I can get new bottoms too? I decided to do some online research.

As I was scouting out my golf options, I came across a website that sold a lot of sports equipment for golf, baseball and pole dancing. Yes, pole dancing–who knew it was a sport! Well, I admit I was intrigued, and I started to read about it. I have to say there is more to pole dancing than meets the eye.

For example, did you know that there is a special grip powder for dancers to ensure that they "stick" to a pole and don't fall off? And it only costs $10.95. How fun would it be to leave pole-dancing grip powder in my bathroom medicine chest and then invite guests over? You know at least one of them will snoop to see what's in there. I bet if I did that, I would soon be despised by every other woman on the block, but on the other hand, I would be pretty damn popular with the men.

While the powder is a must for pole performers, there are times when all the powder in the world is not going to keep a girl attached, so for those slippery moments, there are official pole dancing crash mats. I think the mats are a smart idea. While I have never seen a pole dancer in person, I have seen pictures, and pole dancers are quite the athletic and flexible type. Their routines require a variety of positions, which if not performed correctly, could lead to bodily injury. Nothing takes "the sexy" out of a pole dance like blood pouring from a gaping head wound because the dancer crashed to a hard floor.

Let's see what else do pole dancers need: training gloves, ankle and arm braces, pain relief cream, apparel...yes, I would think the right apparel can make or break a pole dance, and of course, the poles themselves which range in price from $249 for a plain old chrome pole to $499 for a Lil' Mynx Pro Pole in polished stainless steel. Some poles come in colors too which I think would add a festive look to the performance.

I know when people here pole dancing they automatically think smut, but to be honest, the women and men who do this activity have to be in tip-top shape. I have seen pole dancing classes offered (one in the basement of a local church which I thought was odd), and I have been tempted to see what they are all about.

The good thing about going somewhere to take a class is that I would not have to purchase my own pole. It is provided to each student as part of the tuition. I wouldn't mind that as long as I didn't have to share it with someone. To me, a pole is sort of like a toothbrush—only one person should ever use it unless it is disinfected with lots of Purell sanitizer between users. Maybe not Purell as that would make the pole extra slippery, but I guess this is where the grip powder would come into play.

I might really look into one of these classes, but I think I will keep it quiet if I join up. I got enough abuse when I took the belly dancing course, so I think pole dancing might make some of the people I know a little unnerved or worse, interested.

The Life of a Pampered Pet

My daughter played travel softball. When nationals came around, we would always board our German Shepherd Miss Muffie, at The Spa. The place wasn't really called The Spa, but the other parents from the team nicknamed it that because they were jealous of our pooch's accommodations.

The spa was wonderful. Miss Muffie had a private, air-conditioned room with piped in music. We got to choose the music. Since she was of German descent, I opted for Mozart and Beethoven. I thought she would feel more at home with them. The spa had everything that a dog and, truthfully, most humans would want. There was a built-in pool on the premises, plus they had a gourmet chef and massage therapist on staff. Dogs participated in both outside and indoor organized play activities to facilitate group play and encourage camaraderie amongst the guests. I am not making that part up; that is what the brochure said.

So, while we were sitting in ball fields in 100-degree weather, scarfing down hot dogs and pretzels, my dog was at the spa being treated to steak and broiled chicken in her air conditioned suite. And the bill for all this pampering: Well, let's just say my daughter's school tuition seemed like a bargain after a week of dog pampering.

When my second mutt, LuLu, came along, I sent both girls to the spa, but I cut down on the extras so my family and I could afford to do things...like eat. Finally, after Miss Muffie went to that big backyard in the sky and the softball years were over, we decided to use a pet sitter service for the times we had to travel without LuLu and our newest girl beast, Frankie.

Many people through the years mocked my pampering of my pooches, but I am not a rarity when it comes to spoiling my animals. My chiropractor has Stanky the pig. In his prime, Stanky weighed 220 pounds. He was supposed to be a pot belly pig and reach a maximum weight of about 40 pounds, but obviously something went awry. At one time, Stanky thought he was a dog. He would be in the backyard and hear the dogs next door bark, and he would bark. That lasted for a few years until Stanky's dog delusion graduated to a human one.

Stanky has his own room, and he gets not only good table food but a special mix of pig food that my chiropractor has made and shipped to her house. Where my dogs think they are the babies in our family, Stanky thinks he is the man of the house, and he does not like other men coming into his territory. In fact, Stanky does not like my chiropractor to date at all.

I guess it is fair to say that Stanky is a little grouchier now than in past years. He is 16. I am not sure what pig 16 is in human years, but suffice it to say, he is old and has a somewhat entitled attitude. He goes to a piggy camp when my chiropractor has to travel. There he gets his own suite. Some pigs have more dorm-like accommodations with straw beds, but he has his own real bed and blanket, special pig food and hours of "down time" in the meadow.

Pet pampering goes beyond vacation accommodations and into other aspects of daily life. My chiropractor has also paid for the services of an animal communicator to find out what makes Stanky grumpy. Apparently, he gets headaches which can throw off his mood, but on the positive side, the communicator was able to tell my chiropractor that Stanky loves peanut butter and the color purple.

Another friend of mine used to take her cat to an animal psychologist for her emotional issues. She would pay $75 per hour to hear that her cat had anxiety and self-confidence problems. The cat got a prescription for valium. I would have been shocked by this, but my old vet was a believer in legalizing marijuana for the purpose of helping animals in pain. I have to admit that this was where I drew the line. If anyone was going to get legalized pot, it was going to be me.

I guess it is safe to say that many of us treat our animals better than we do some of our own family members. Is it bad? No. My pets give me companionship and joy and on cold nights when my husband won't let me put my cold feet underneath him, my dogs warm my feet. So, for that reason alone, they deserve to be pampered.

I think if there is such a thing as reincarnation, I am going to sign up to be a dog when my time comes. However, with my luck, instead of getting placed in a pampering family, I might wind up in some third world country where dog meat is the most common food staple. Perhaps, I should re-think this and consider coming back as something higher up on the food chain.

He Might Only Have Eyes for Me But Where Are His Ears?

During one of my insomnia nights, I decided to grab my laptop and read some online news. There was an interesting article (and I cannot find it now, so I have to wonder if I dreamed the whole thing) on the frequency differences between the voices of men and the voices of women. Apparently, a male voice ranges between 100 to 150 Hz while a female voice ranges between170 to 220 Hz.

For those of you, like myself, who did not major in voice frequency in college, Hz or Hertz (not the car rental company) is the unit of measure of frequency and is defined as the number of complete cycles per second. When applied to voices, Hz helps to register things like pitch. I think I did learn about the Hz unit in a Physics class somewhere between the 10th grade and my college graduation, but I truly believe that the knowledge I gained during those years has somehow leaked out of my brain and is lost forever.

Anyway, after stumbling through this article, I did start to think about the whole difference in frequency thing, and I started to wonder if it was behind my husband's lack of listening skills where I am concerned. I don't mean to pick on him, but he has this nasty habit I call "tunnel hearing". Similar to tunnel vision, which is when a person can only see what is directly in front of him, my version of tunnel hearing is when a person can only *hear* what is directly in front of him. I can literally stand two feet to the side of my husband and ask him a question, and he will not respond. He is not being rude or insensitive; he cannot hear me. At one point in our marriage, I made him go see a hearing specialist. I thought all the years of listening to hard rock had finally taken its toll, but he passed the tests with flying colors. Go figure. So, I started to ask my friends if they experienced the same phenomenon as I do. This is what I found out.

First: A lot of men do suffer from tunnel hearing. It's so prevalent that I am thinking of starting a non-profit for it. The funny and puzzling thing about tunnel hearing is that it only affects the communication between men and women. Men hear other men when they are right next to them; they can hear other men across a crowded bar; and they can even hear other men across a packed stadium during the Super Bowl. But a wife standing six inches to his side has not a chance in hell of being heard.

Second: Most men can adjust their hearing to their wives' voice frequencies so that they can hear certain statements – even at a distance - and are able to respond to these statements without any prodding. These statements are (and not in any particular order):

1. I had a slight incident with your car today that requires some minor bodywork.
2. The Cable is out, and they said it might take a day or two for them to get it back.
3. Do you want to have sex tonight?

As you might guess, number three is the statement that requires the least voice frequency sensitivity. I found out from my totally unscientific and undocumented research that men can be lost in the woods, miles from civilization, but when they hear those words, even if they are unsure if they are meant for them, they will find their way home without help from a compass or GPS. The funny thing about voice frequency is that it never seems to affect single men. They seem to hear everything their girlfriends or dates say to them. Unmarried men never ask, "Did you say something?" Or "I did not hear you. What was that?" And the single women never seem to have to say, "Did you hear me? Or my personal favorite,"What did I just say to you? Do you even know?"

I have a theory on this married man - single man thing too in case anyone was wondering. I think when men get married and put on a wedding ring, the metal in the ring interacts with voice frequency and causes the tunnel hearing effect. I think it is a chemistry or physics thing. No ring, no problem; wedding ring,big problem. Someday, they may find a cure for tunnel hearing. Until then, I will just bide my time and repeat my questions over and over again and be happy when I get a response.

Trying to Get Men to Date

I was helping a guy friend fill out a profile for a dating site. This was a new experience for me. Usually, I am called in to help my female friends build a profile that would attract a man who is, as my one girlfriend put it, "A Johnny Depp, Bill Gates and Tom Brady combo." Yes, I think she does drink or perhaps listens to too many Law of Attraction CDs, but whatever gets her going in the morning, I am okay with.

Anyway, I noticed my guy friend was a lot less thoughtful over his answers to the profile questions than my female friends. To questions such as "Where do you see yourself in five years?" my girlfriends struggle to create answers that reflect their desire to be in a long-time relationship or married without sounding needy or desperate. However, to this specific inquiry, my guy friend answered "fishing alone in my own boat on the ocean…alone."

Keeping in mind that he was new to the dating site world, I told him in the most patient tone I could muster, that using the word *alone* twice did not exactly scream, "I am okay with commitment." He just shrugged his shoulders and gave me permission to answer the question as long as I was honest and didn't make it sound like he wanted to be in a long-term relationship anytime soon.

I could do nothing but stare at him and shake my head. Before we finished this profile for this particular dating site, I decided to research other sites to see if there was one more suitable to his lifestyle. If there was a site, "Hookers for love" he would have signed up right away, but I tried to explain that if he wanted a nice woman, and by that I mean one who he doesn't have to pay to talk dirty to him, he should refrain from the more "open" sites.

Along with the usual dating sites, I stumbled across several religious-based sites such as Christiansingles.com where you put your search for the right mate into God's hands. Now, this I thought was a little puzzling. If God is so intent on finding my friend a match, why doesn't he just lead him to the intended woman? Why does he need a third party? Why must my friend fill out membership information to dig through thousands of women profiles to find Ms. Right? If God really wanted to make my friend a match, couldn't he just plop the perfect mate into the middle of his bedroom and say, "Here she is! I picked her out for you myself!" I would think a third-party dating site is a little insulting to the Big Matchmaker in the sky. Oh, and for anyone who likes the idea of faith-based dating, but you are not a Christian, do not fret. There were other faith-based sites to choose from such as jdate.com, singlemuslim.com, wiccanpassions.com – and let's not leave out the atheists or agnostics – freethinkermatch.com. See, something for everyone.

Finally, we got through the profile, and now instead of sounding like a guy who might go into convulsions at the mere utterance of the word "girlfriend", my friend sounded like a relatively nice guy who on paper is considerate, open-minded and rich. Well, at least affluent. Hell, he owns his own condo and car and he gets a paycheck every week, and except for that arrest for public intoxication a decade ago, he is what most mothers would refer to as "a nice catch" as long as they don't get to know him too well.

We moved onto the last phase of this project: the photo. I suggested that he shave his day's worth of stubble. He thought it made him look sexy; I thought it made him look like a sexual predator. So, he shaved. Next, I suggested a nice golf shirt instead of the tee shirt that displayed the saying, "Route 69 – Going down?" I thought that this tee shirt gave women the wrong impression.

We snapped the picture and put it up on the website and guess what? He got six inquiries in less than 24 hours. Now, my friend is happy that I budded into his life. Will he marry any of these women? Hell, no. As he says, "Fool me once, shame on me; fool me twice or three times – that just makes me really stupid." But, he might find a nice person to have a relationship with, and that would make me happy. I have to be honest; I do sleep a little better knowing that I took a man who lived a life of single bliss and immersed him without an oxygen tank into the chaotic and traumatic world of committed relationships.

Leaving the Pasties Behind

Learning annexes always send me brochures and schedules on inexpensive classes I can take in my free time. I normally circle about five courses that interest me from automobile repair to past life regression. Yes, I go the gamut. Unfortunately, my work schedule rarely meshes with any of the courses, so the brochure usually winds up in the trash along with my dreams of being able to change my own oil or my desire to learn about my former life as a prostitute for the Confederacy during the American Civil War. Yes, a psychic once told me that I walked the streets ready to please the South's finest. That must explain my weakness for fried chicken and men in gray uniforms or suits.

The latest brochure came a few days ago, and it came from a local theater that offered classes to adults and kids. The kids' classes were the typical *Public Speaking and Acting* or *Learning to Develop Characters*. But the adult section had something unique: *Introduction to Burlesque*. Of course, this class caught my eye. Well, what do you expect? I was a hooker in an earlier life, so it makes sense that burlesque would capture my interest in this life. Anyway, the class tuition included the history, theory and practical applications of burlesque and pasties! You got your own pasties! I was intrigued.

As I read on, the class included six-weeks of burlesque dance instruction and the final class was a recital which was open to the public. My first question to this was: who goes to a burlesque recital? I would think that burlesque is a type of entertainment that does not work with amateurs. I would assume that those who like burlesque, would want to see "good-body" burlesque not "middle-aged women who thought Pilates was boring and were looking for something more exciting burlesque. If I didn't have to dance in front of people who could only afford to see free burlesque and the pasties were for practice only at home, I might have signed up for the class. However, since I cannot even get the guts to wear a two-piece bathing suit in public, I'm pretty sure dancing around with just pasties on in front of the neighborhood men was out of the question.

Sometimes when an idea is pretty farfetched, it tends to loiter in my brain a few days. I think that is my head's way of trying to get me to like the idea. So, during the days when the burlesque class was squatting in my mind, I happened to have an appointment with my chiropractor. While we were chit chatting, I mentioned the burlesque class to which she responded.

"Oh my God, I have been to one of their recitals!"

"What the hell were you doing at a free burlesque recital?"

"A guy took me. It was our first date," she said matter-of-factly.

"What kind of kinky guy takes you to a burlesque class recital on a first date?"

"I probably won't see him again. I was a little put off."

It turned out she was the only woman watching the recital, and the guy she was with didn't really care that she was uncomfortable, which made us wonder why he took her to this show. We listed many reasons for his choice of venue, some were funny, and some were deeply disturbing. In the end, we decided she probably wouldn't date him again.

Well, a few good things came out of this chiropractic session. My neck doesn't hurt, I no longer have any desire to dance around in pasties...while attending a burlesque class anyway, and we made a new list of traits that my chiropractor should look for in men. All in all - not a bad hour's work.

Small Feet Won't Get Me Into the Army

I have small feet. On the hottest day of the year when feet are supposed to expand and swell the most, I can maybe make it into a size 5. Why is my foot size important you may ask? Well, it has impacted my life over the years.

I never really knew my small foot was a big deal until the third grade. Before that, people would comment on my petite feet, but I never thought much of it. However, it was during the third grade that my school hired a new gym teacher. He had recently been discharged from the Marine Corps and had, what would now be labeled as "issues". He called us all by our last names and separated the class into squads. We had to address him as "Sir", and when, he asked a question we had to yell in response, "Sir, Yes Sir!" or "Sir, No Sir!" Even at the tender age of eight, I knew something was wrong when boys and girls were fighting trying to get promoted to corporal and sergeant, and each gym class started with all of us singing *From the Halls of Montezuma.*

I would tell my parents about gym class and they would say, "Oh, he was in Viet Nam? Your three cousins were in Viet Nam. Maybe they were friends. Be kind."

In my parents' defense, back then, no one questioned teachers. No other parent seemed to mind either, but one day, the school principal happened to come into the gym during drills. She must have seen something she did not like because when fourth grade began, I had a kinder and gentler woman gym teacher.

I swear I am getting to the point, and here it is: It was the shell-shocked marine who first made an issue of my small feet. In fact, it was my small feet that prevented my promotion to the rank of corporal in the Third Grade Armed Forces Auxiliary Unit. To this day, I am not sure what our unit could do legally, but I think by the time the year ended, we were prepared for armed combat. During one of our endurance and survival classes, I tripped and fell to the ground. Of course, the marine noticed and started to yell.

"What is wrong with you? Are your shoelaces untied?" Then, he looked down at my feet, and he was genuinely shocked. "What do you call those things?"

"My feet, Sir," I dutifully answered.

"Those are not feet! You could not be a marine with those feet! You can't lead a platoon with those feet!"

Being young and stupid, I was insulted by his remarks. Later, I realized that if the government in all its wisdom insisted on war, kept the draft and expanded it to include women, I probably would get a pass.

Now, let's fast forward to the start of high school. I went to an all-girl prep school. Before freshman year, my Mom and I went to the uniform store to get my freshman duds. My two sisters had gone through the school before me, so I sort of knew what to expect, but we soon learned that the incoming freshman class had one more item on the uniform list: shoes – bumper toe saddle shoes to be specific.

The salesman at the uniform shoe store put my foot in the metal measuring gadget and said, "The shoes do not come in a 13 1/2. The smallest is a size two. We can give you the size two and some foam rubber wedges to stuff the toes."

For two years, I walked around with my toes clenched around wads of foam rubber so my shoes would not fall off. Fortunately, junior year brought about upperclassmen uniform changes. The uniform shoe was the same as one of the local grammar schools, and they had the smaller sizes for me to order. My feet never felt so good. I had forgotten what it's like to spread out my toes.

Since then, the entire small foot thing has proved to be a mixed blessing. For instance, today I can buy children's Uggs boots for about $40 cheaper than adult-size boots. However, not all children's shoes fit the style demands of adult feet. For instance, children's dress shoes lack the sophistication of a sexy slingback. Little girls tend to want their shoes to have lots of sparkles, Barbies or at least a Disney princess on them. Nothing screams "Don't hire me!" on a job interview like The Little Mermaid glittering on your toes.

In the full scheme of life, a small foot is a minor nuisance at best, and a nuisance I have unfortunately, passed onto my daughter.

However, now there is internet shopping. There is a rule of thumb we follow when it comes to shopping for shoes on line. As soon as you see a shoe you like, order it immediately. Why? Because every other small-footed woman is combing the same sites looking for the same shoes as you are, and there are not that many shoes that are size five or smaller out there. So, if you snooze, you lose and you are destined either to walk around barefoot or to wear shoes with the word *Barbie* painted on them.

What is My Fantasy Job?

Each day, my email is filled with educational opportunities that promise to put me on the path to financial success and personal satisfaction. I have to admit that some of these emails grab my attention. Do you know that in a few short months, I can be an x-ray technician, bartender or social worker? I don't know how these "schools" who send these emails know that it will only take me "a few short months" to complete their rigorous academic requirements, but I suspect that if I am willing to pay their tuition, I might even be able to get a medical degree.

Anyway, as I stared at the possible list of careers I could pursue, I started to ponder my dream jobs. So, below is a list of careers that I have often thought would be fun to take on.

Truck Driver: I have always longed for the freedom of the open road. I could see me sitting behind the wheel of one of those 18-wheeler things and having a grand old time on the CB. Do truckers still use CBs or are they cell phone people now? I hope there are CBs. I would love to have a cool or scary identity – I guess the correct term is "handle" – such as Mama Frizz or PMS Queen or Man killer. Nothing would get in my way except some of the idiot drivers on the New Jersey Turnpike or state troopers who do not appreciate my affinity for tailgating and blowing my big trucker horn at old people who refuse to go more than 45 MPH in the center lane. The only trucking gig I wouldn't do is ice road driving. I saw that TV show, and there is no way that I am driving across frozen lakes and rivers to deliver auto parts to some car dealer in East Snowshoe, Alaska.

Trapeze artist: I don't know why this would be so much fun for me except that I could legitimately sing– and feel free to sing along – *I fly through the air with the greatest of ease, I'm the amazing chick on that flying trapeze.* I do have some knowledge of the circus life. I interview traveling circus people for a trade magazine often, and they are so interesting. Plus, I would think that if you go around telling men you are a trapeze artist, you never lack a date. I don't know why this is true, but men just seem to love trapeze artists. Me, I go gaga over someone who can offer a steady income and a walk-in closet, but hey, everyone is different.

Sports team mascot (specifically the Philly Phanatic): This is truly my dream job! Imagine how it would be? I could put on a costume and gyrate in a way that would get me arrested if I was not in that costume. I could stand on top of the Phillies dugout and yell at umpires and opposing players without worrying about security escorting me from the park. This is like dying and going to heaven. The Phanatic persona combines celebrity clout with anonymity which I have to think leads to a lot of perks wherever I go as long as I am in costume.

Casino Security Person in Las Vegas: I want this job because there is no better place to people watch than Vegas, and no job allows you more access to people than security at a casino. When I was in Vegas, I started to chat with a man who was in casino security. He could read people so clearly, and he was telling me about the characters he sees. "It's a novel waiting to happen," he said. "I don't even need security cameras to know what they are up to. I have been in this job so long, that by looking at people, I can tell if they are criminals, cheaters, etc. When they come here, they just let it show." To have that kind of insight on human nature would be amazing to me, plus maybe I could learn to count cards and finally win big.

Baywatch Babe: I can hear women everywhere asking "Why? Why this job?" Because simply, I would be at the beach all day and this to me would be great. Okay, it's also the boobs! For five minutes, I would love to know what it is like to have those boobs, and find out if they do really help one float. The other perks of the job is no office work and no boring work clothes. The downside to being a Baywatch Babe: riptides and sharks.

Third string quarterback in the NFL: If I were a man, this would be my top job. Why? I would get the league minimum of more than $500,000 per year; I would rarely have to play a single game because there is a star QB and the second-stringer hoping the star gets hurt so he can become the first-stringer; and since I would probably not have to see a moment of action, I would have no long-term, chronic health issues. Best of all, when someone asks what I did for a living, I would get to say truthfully, "I am an NFL quarterback." As a guy, I bet that would make me a chick magnet. As a woman, I have no shot at this job, so I will save it as a possibility for my next life.

Food tester for famous bakery chefs: Nothing gives me more joy than desserts. I am a cookie eating, cake-loving, ice cream-a-holic who lives for sweet treats. As a pastry tester for the famous chefs of the world, I would get my share of not only everyday desserts but the desserts that only royalty enjoys. I don't know how one gets a job as pastry tester, and I did not see a category for it on Monster.com, but if anyone has an "in" on this career, please let me know.

Will Video Poker Make Me Rich?

I live about an hour or so from Atlantic City. I only realized I lived that close about three years ago. Usually, if I headed to the beach, I headed to the water and sand and never gave a thought about the bright lights of the casinos, so I sort of forgot the entire city was even there.

One Saturday morning, my husband suggested that we take a ride to Atlantic City and have some fun. I am always up for an adventure, so I agreed. I wasn't exactly sure what I would play in the casino. I knew how to play poker; I played in college, but it was a very low stress game. The games were always coed, and if you were a player of the female persuasion and you lost, you only had to put on a sad face and the guys would worry that you were going to cry, and they would just say "Oh, forget it, you don't have to pay me." I went three years without losing a dime in poker. It was not a good training camp for the real game or for life either.

You can understand why, with my poker background, I didn't want to play with "pros" in the casino. I just think a sad face would not work on the real poker crowd plus I never developed a knack for the whole check, call, and raise process. So, my husband told me about video poker, and I thought this is something I could get into.

We went to one of the Trump casinos, and when we got inside, my husband wanted to play black jack. I sent him on his merry way, so I could explore. I found this fun video poker game that spun like the slot machines. A nice gentleman offered me a seat next to him and gave me a quick lesson on "Spin Poker". I inserted a $20 bill, and my first hand popped up. I selected the cards I wanted to play; I hit spin, and I got four aces. I decided I liked this game.

When the aces hit, I made sure I didn't scream or carry on, but unintentionally, I let out a little squeal. Unfortunately, an old witch on the opposite side of my new gentleman friend complained out loud at my showy and inconsiderate emotion. I am not calling her a witch because she was mean (which she was). I am calling her a witch because she had all these little troll dolls and voodoo things lined up on top of her machine and kept asking them to help her. Until that day, I was unaware that there was a deity devoted to gambling. I must have missed that chapter in catechism class.

I continued to play, but after a while the game started to get boring. Then, it happened. I hit the spin button and five twos came up or four twos and a joker--something like that. The token counter kept going up and up and bells went off, and I knew it was a good thing, but I didn't know how good it was. My gentleman friend hugged me and was screaming with delight for me, and the old witch gave him the dirtiest look, and I said,

"Maybe we shouldn't be so loud."

"Why? Because of her?" he asked. "Ignore the old bat and enjoy the win! Besides, she's my wife."

Yes, there we had it. Another marriage made in heaven. With that stunning revelation, I decided to call my husband and tell him of my windfall.

"I think we are rich! I got a lot of twos, and the machine is making a lot of noise. Can you come here now?"

The machine was still tallying my total when I saw my husband coming up the escalator.

"Do you think it's over a $100,000?" I asked

"Uh, no, but it's over $1,000 dollars, and that's really good."

The precise number came to be $2,550 when all was said and done. I have to admit that I was pretty happy. The old witch stormed off, and her husband let her, and the casino people came over and congratulated me. It was lots of fun.

Once, I had the cash in hand, I took my winnings over to the Coach store in the nearby mall. There, I bought my daughter's Christmas present with some of the winnings and treated my husband to lunch at a nice restaurant that overlooked the water. When I got home, I socked the rest of the cash in the bank.

Later, I called my Dad and told him that I had won, and after warm congratulations, he warned me that people do not win all the time, but guess what? I went back three more times in the next six months and won each time: $250, $400 and $800.

However, the fourth time we went back, the spell was broken, and I lost. The magic of the spin video poker game died, and I have not wanted to go back since.

Will I try again? I guess. It's not anything I feel an urgency to do, but maybe when we head to the beach for a day, we will swing past Atlantic City and I can take another stab at winning our millions. Someone has to win, so why not me?

Food, Hormones…and I Forget

I want to believe with every fiber of my being that people break into my house and steal my food. This is the best explanation I have for why my refrigerator is empty. I go shopping almost every day, but every night when I go to make lunches for the following day, there is no food. I am out of everything. I have to believe that I am the target of a well-established food burglary ring because the only other explanation I have is that I forget to buy what I need when I go to the grocery store. And that can't be true because as I tell everyone, I have an amazing memory.

I can tell you what you wore when you came to my house for dinner 15 years ago. I can tell you a couple's chosen wedding song for every wedding I have been to throughout my life. I can recall that Lisa Lawrence's birthday is March 3rd, and FYI, Lisa Lawrence was my best friend in kindergarten back at PS 138 in the Bronx. See, these long ago details do not escape my steel-trap brain, but the fact that I am out of milk or turkey for lunches slips through the seams of my grey matter quickly.

Okay, I will admit that I have a short-term memory deficit, and like most women, I will chalk it up to hormones. I pretty much chalk up all my faults to hormones. My hormones are responsible for everything from my lead foot on the highway to my inability to mow the lawn in a straight line. Yes, if I allow them, hormones are my excuse for every flaw I own. And to be honest, I think I deserve that excuse, and I think all women do as well.

To counter my short-term memory issues, I keep lists. The problem with the lists is that I forget where I put them so I don't take them with me when I go to the store. Without my lists, I tend to wander aimlessly down the aisles trying to remember why I was there; hoping something from the shelves will jump out and jog my memory. Do I remember? Never. And what is worse is that I wind up spending $150 on crap that I know was not on my list but looked good on the special display that day.

I think stores in general rely on the hormonal upheaval of women. There must be some kind of retail term for sucking in perimenopausal females when a store wants them to make certain purchases. I wonder if there is some kind of scanner that goes off and alerts store management when a woman high on hormones comes through the door. Now, that I think about it, there are a lot of women hanging out in the candy and baking aisles. I used to think that there was a low blood sugar cluster in my area, but maybe it's just a lot of hormones fermenting. It could be that stores have figured out the hormone thing, and this is why there is always a two-for-one promotion or a buy-three-and-get-a-fourth-free sale on the chocolate or bakery items. Maybe, I have fallen victim to this retail conspiracy against perimenopausal women and this is why I felt the need to convert one entire cupboard in my kitchen for my chocolate stash.

Wow, I got really off topic here, but a piece of dark chocolate does sound really good right now. Anyway, I think I might have to write a piece on the fluctuating hormones of women and the resulting short-term memory loss. Oh wait, I think I just did, Sorry, I forgot.

The Almost Demise of a Woodchuck

I live in a development on a half-acre of land in suburban Philadelphia. While I may not have to worry about bears or lions showing up to devour my family, I do at times have my own version of Wild Kingdom in my backyard.

Recently, I had to do phone interview with a company CEO for an article I was writing. With my office in my home, I try to make sure my dogs cannot be heard by another party when I am on the phone. When the weather is good, "the girls" play in the yard or sit in the shade and just enjoy their near Utopian existence so I can work in peace. I do check on them periodically. While my dogs love their yard, they have been known on occasion to dig tunnels under the fence and make a break for it. Well, it's my big dog, Frankie, who is the instigator in this activity. My little pooch, LuLu, goes along with Frankie out of peer pressure.

Anyway, I was doing the phone interview with this CEO, and I heard a weird sound emanating from the yard. My first thought was that one of my dogs was stuck trying to escape, but the sounds were not the sounds that either of my dogs would make. They were high-pitched, disturbing screams that sounded as if they might be coming from my neighbor's house. With phone in hand, and interviewee still on the line, I headed toward the source of the screeching noise. I opened the backdoor, and immediately my heart began to race. I could see my dogs by my vegetable gardens, and they were engaged in hand-to-hand combat with a woodchuck or ground hog or some creature like that.

I will admit that I do not know the difference between many of these critters. I can identify skunks, raccoons and deer, but this is where my expertise ends. This furry creature did resemble the ground hog Punxsutawney Phil, who comes out every February 2nd to tell us if spring is on the way. However, this animal was a lot bigger, and he did not look quite as happy as Phil since each of my dogs had one of its legs in their mouths, and the animal was about to be drawn and quartered.

You might not know this about me, but I don't do "calm" well. In fact, panic is pretty much my strong suit. I dropped the phone and started to wave my arms in a wild motion hoping I would grab the attention of my dogs who seemed intent on pulling apart this rodent-looking creature. When my flailing failed to distract the pooches, I started to yell. "WHAT THE HELL ARE YOU DOING? GET AWAY! STOP IT! LET GO OF THOSE PAWS! DON'T YOU DARE EAT THAT ANIMAL!"

Then I heard this voice screaming at me from a distance, and I realized I left the man I was interviewing on the phone. "Donna, where are you? Are you okay? Should I call 911?"

I ran back to the phone which was lying in the grass and in a surprisingly professional voice I said, "My dogs are tearing apart some kind of animal. Could you hold just one minute?"

The man had to think I was a psycho, but I didn't even wait for an answer. I threw the phone back on the lawn and ran to get the garden hose. I turned on the water and dragged the hose back to where the animal tug of war was taking place. In my haste, I tripped and fell and yes, I got boo boos which resulted in another set of colorful expletives. To my credit, my bloody knees did not deter me from saving that bold critter that came into my yard to feed on my garden.

I felt like a super cop in one of those action movies. From the ground, I hoisted myself up on my scraped elbows, and with the poise of a sharpshooter, I took aim with the hose and blasted both dogs and the critter. All three were pretty shocked when that water hit them. The dogs, who hate the hose, immediately let go of the animal and took off to hide behind trees. Still trembling with fear, the alien critter stared at me but made no attempt to leave the yard.

I took a closer look at the creature and noticed there was no blood. This animal wasn't hurt. So, I turned the hose on it again, and it scurried under my neighbor's fence. Then, I took the girls inside and gave them tons of doggie breath fresheners.

As I was lying in bed that night, I suddenly realized that the phone was still outside on the lawn, and I never got back to the CEO and most likely he heard the whole chaotic event. I got up, located the phone in the grass, and made peace with the fact that I would be doing a lot of explaining to a lot of people come morning.

The Devil Made Me Do It

"The devil led me in that direction." Yep, that was the excuse a friend of mine's ex-boyfriend used when she confronted him with his cheating ways. I have to admit that when my friend told me this gem of an excuse, I was stunned by his creative attempt to skirt responsibility. I would have accepted, but not approved of, the usual excuses which include *You don't understand me*; *I am feeling smothered in this relationship*; and my personal favorite, *It meant nothing to me even though I have been sleeping with her for about a month.*

But the devil thing was a new one, and I have to give this guy credit as this excuse took a lot of chutzpah to utter. Imagine calling in Satan to take the rap. I handed my friend tissues, a chunk of chocolate cake, some of the jello shots I keep in reserve for my girlfriend-in-need situations, and then I sang the traditional break-up song, "He is scum, and you are better off without him!" But even as I was singing the "scum" tune over and over and doing all the correct post-breakup rituals, I could not help but chuckle at what was going on inside my head. I began to imagine how the devil decided that this guy would be a good choice to prod into cheating. How desperate is the Prince of the Underworld?

Picture the scene: The guy with horns and a pitchfork is scouring the Earth looking for a dupe to continue his evil work when he spots Joe Schmuck Boyfriend sitting in his truck.

"Ah, this guy looks like he has possibilities. He has that dumb look that says he might be distracted easily."

To get his plan moving along, the devil transforms himself into a middle-aged woman looking for romance. When the dupe goes to his local watering hole for a quick beer, he runs into the she-devil who is waiting to bait the trap.

"Hi, you look like a nice guy. Let's have sex," the demonette suggests.

"Okay, that sounds like fun," the dupe agrees after a millisecond of consideration.

And when the deed is done, the accommodating woman turns back into the Satan we all know and love, and informs the dupe that he has been led astray.

"But I have a girlfriend who I have been dating for over a year! How could you do this to me?" The dupe asks in horror.

"Don't worry about it. Just tell her that the devil led you in this direction. She will believe you."

When I told my now, jello-shot-calmed-friend of my imaginative version of the whole devil thing, she started to giggle.

"So, this idiot is the best the devil can do?" She asked. "I guess he just preys on the stupid."

And with that observation, I knew my girlfriend would be okay especially since she admitted that this was the fourth time he cheated on her. I tried not to look at her as if she was from out of space, but I had to wonder where my friend's usual good judgment was hiding when she met this guy. I also wondered how the dupe gave into cheating so easily. So, being the intrepid journalist I am, who also had her fair share of jello shots, I called him. Yes, I did. And when he answered, I said in my most professional tone,

"Hey, you are a moron who has no idea what you lost, but that is a topic for another time. I need to know how you knew it was the devil forcing you to cheat."

"Well," and he answered me seriously, "I only cheat when I feel temptation, and temptation is the devil's tool. So, if I get the urge to cheat, it's not my fault; it's the devil's doing. I am the victim, and she should understand and forgive me. I can't help if the devil calls to me."

Uh huh. I was now getting a clearer picture of this guy.

"Okay, we may be done here. Have a nice life and you know what? You are right. You are too good for her. Go find someone else, someone better for you - far, far away."

He seemed pleased I took his side, and thanked me for my concern. After I hung up, I looked at my friend and said, "Yea. He really wasn't good for you. I just have a feeling there would have been a lot more trouble down the road."

"Really? I am thinking that too. He was fun for a while."

I could do nothing but nod. Fortunately, the devil and the dupe disappeared from my friend's life forever. Did she mourn this loss of a boyfriend? For about a week. She met another nice man who had no relationship with the devil whatsoever, so I feel pretty good about this one. But just in case the dark prince returns, I have chocolate cake, tissues and jello shots ready and waiting.

The Collateral Damage of a Friend's Breakup

One of my friends was unceremoniously dumped over a Burger King lunch. The week or so before this traumatic event, she was convinced that her beloved was going to pop the question, and he did, but it was the wrong question. She was ready to hear "Will you marry me?" What came out of his mouth was "Don't you think this relationship has run its course?"

At the beginning, I was there with Kleenex, chocolate, a midnight cheesesteak run to Pat's in South Philly, and of course, a good amount of wine. Then as the days wore on, my teary-eyed friend went from heartbroken to belligerent. At first, I thought it was healthy for her to let go of all the venom trapped in her broken heart, but then her anger took a weird turn: It took aim at me.

We were out to lunch. I was in my jeans and a tee shirt. It's not like we were going to a four-star restaurant. We were scarfing down spinach dip or whatever the dip was at Applebee's and talking about her defunct relationship when I said,

"You know, out there is the right guy for you. Just wait and see." A harmless bit of encouragement I thought. To which she responded in a rather hostile tone,

"There is no one for me; my chance has passed!" I could see that her eyeballs were now darting back and forth inside their sockets. Then her voice climbed about two octaves, and she screamed for the entire restaurant to hear, "AND IF

YOUR HUSBAND WAS GONE, THERE WOULD BE
NO ONE FOR YOU EITHER! NO ONE! YOU ARE IN
YOUR FORTIES - WHO WOULD WANT *YOU*?" (The
emphasis being on the *you*.)

Well, that was a tad insulting. I didn't know whether to
hold her hand, get her a Xanax, or throw the freaking dip in
her face! In truth, my only response to this was, and please
understand I was somewhat in shock and a little
embarrassed as eyes were now on our table, "Why? I clean
up good."

It is no surprise that I paid that check as fast as I could,
threw her in the car and sped to her office where I pushed
her out onto the sidewalk. She didn't even have a chance to
say goodbye or shut the passenger side door fully. I pulled
the door shut myself at the first red light I came to. I then
went to the nearest CVS and bought a boatload of wrinkle
cream.

I'll admit she rocked my confidence, but my feelings of
insecurity were soon surpassed by feelings of anger. What
was weird is that I was not angry at her; instead, I was
angry at the entire male population, who according to my
friend, had already decided to reject me. Right away, I
knew someone was going to have to pay for that comment,
and unfortunately, that person was going to have to be my
husband. When he walked in the door that night, I greeted
him with this question.

"If you were dead, do you think another man would find
me attractive?"

He hesitated before he spoke and joked, "Yes, you still have all my life insurance money."

"You're an ass!" I snapped.

Sensing trouble ahead, he tried to backpedal to avoid a fight he did not see coming. The man did attend military school, so he understands the need to diminish the effects of the element of surprise as quickly as possible.

"What kind of question is that? Of course, someone would," he said lovingly. "By the way, why do I have to be dead? Why can't we be divorced in this scenario?"

"Someone? Maybe one guy?" I said skirting his question. "That's it?"

"No, no *lots* of men. I am sure, he said in an exasperated tone. "Do I get to know why I am in trouble?"

You know, I always wonder at these moments in our marriage why my husband did not divorce me years ago. As an engineer, that would have been the logical thing to do. Many of his engineer friends have spouses in equally logical professions who bring home much bigger paychecks than me. It probably would have been in his best interest to look for a spouse elsewhere.

So, I explained to him about the lunch. I have to say, he was pretty perturbed with my friend and her comments. He thought it was callous and totally not true, and he also thought that an understanding approach was going to get him out of any potential argument with me.

Yeah, he was wrong. In fact, for an entire week, he was not out of the woods. Why? Because he was still a male, and my ego was still bruised, and he had to make up for all the future rejection of his entire gender. I did learn three things from this hurtful experience. First: Not all men are to blame for the bad actions of a few (This lesson will fluctuate over time depending on the situation and my hormone levels). Second: I will never go to a restaurant or any other public venue with that friend again without a written note from her therapist that she is taking her medication; and finally, if I was that guy she was dating, I would have dumped her in Burger King too.

Can the Navy Seals Train my Dog?

In reading the news, I came upon the hundredth or so article about the raid that killed Osama Bin Laden. One of the most interesting reports focused on the dog that was part of the raid. Apparently, this dog, which is either a Belgian Malinois or a German Shepherd, was strapped to a Navy Seal while they were both lowered from a helicopter, and according to the story, it was indeed this pooch's snout that sniffed out the illusive Bin Laden in his lair. In order to shield the dog from the limelight and the thousands of interview requests from journalists and talk show hosts, the government has decided to keep the brave dog's identity a secret. I guess they need the dog to stay focused and not fall into the ego trap of believing his or her own press.

Okay, I need to sign up my lab/shepherd mix, Frankie, for the Navy Seals. She obviously needs a stronger hand in the obedience training department. The military dog can sniff out fugitives and really big bad guys in the midst of gun battles and whatever other chaos goes on, and my 90-pound moose will not even sit and stay on command. Yes, the military dog will be awarded the highest of honors for helping the navy conduct one of the most complicated and heroic raids in history, and I can't get my dog to come to me from the back of the yard when I call her. The Osama-sniffing dog can bite through steel-enforced clothing using his or her titanium teeth and my dog wants her hot dogs cut up into little pieces so she doesn't choke. (I don't know if she's afraid of choking but she won't eat hot dogs whole)

Yes, I used to think it was the dog's fault why she didn't listen, but I am starting to wonder if it's me. I am going to call the Navy Seals and see if they want to try their hand at training my dog. They don't have to keep her. I will happily take her back, but when she returns from boot camp, I want a dog that is brave, trustworthy and obedient. If that is too much to ask, can she at least become a dog that gives me back my side of the bed?

How to Avoid Guests and Other Paranormal Fun

Last night while flipping through the channels, I came upon the show, *Celebrity Ghost Stories*. I have to say Hollywood's stars have some pretty creepy experiences to share.

During this episode, I watched Christopher Knight, Margaret Cho and some unfamiliar actress tell their real-life ghostly encounters. Are these things real? Sure, why not? Who am I to judge? I plan on coming back and wreaking havoc on unsuspecting living people. Why? Because I can, and there are some people who I would like to drive to the brink of insanity – I think it would be fun.

Personally, I think ghosts are okay guests as long as they are not ghosts who insist on taking over the house or the person living in the house as was the case with the unfriendly demons in *The Exorcist* or *Amityville Horror*. The celebrity ghostly encounters got me thinking about house hauntings, so I have come up with a few rules which should help both celebrities and regular people avoid paranormal and possession mayhem.

Don't move into a house with a history - By history I mean "crime" history. Murder, suicide--anything violent is a sign that this house might not be for you. Okay, say the seller forgets to disclose the fact that six people were murdered in the house, and you move in only to discover that a few weeks down the road, your five-year-old kid drops the F-bomb constantly while his head makes 360-degree spins. Should you be alarmed?

Yes, you should be very alarmed, and you need to leave. This is my problem with these shows. People stay in houses even after a once sweet spouse grows horns on his or her head and displays glowing red eyes which were once baby blue. They blame the demon transformation on everything from the weather to eating bad fish. I am as skeptical as the next person, but if you are alone in a room and a loud, angry voice yells, "GET OUT!" do yourself a favor and get out! Get out as fast as your little feet can take you. Those stupid Amityville people waited until blood started to stream down the walls and for the husband to turn homicidal before they abandoned ship. Here's a rule of thumb: If your spouse is coming at you with a hatchet, you might have waited too long.

Don't move into a house or apartment where the rent should be $4000 a month but the landlord charges you $200 per month - Let me just say this straight out: No one wants to give you a great deal on rent because you are special. You are not *that* special – no one is. A really good deal on rent is obviously a sign that the apartment was a site for satanic worship. I learned this fact from watching *Rosemary's Baby.* If someone wants you to lease an apartment that badly, something is definitely wrong. That 80-plus percent-rent discount (I don't know if that is the right percentage as I suck at math so all you engineers can figure that out for me) is not because there is a roach or rodent problem. No, that big discount should be a red flag, a warning that you will be sharing that apartment with someone who is not of this world.

Do not buy a home that has had 10 owners in the past year - If a house spits out owners this quickly, there is a problem. And while I think that owners are legally supposed to disclose all problems with the house, they tend to fib a bit when it comes to ghosts. I guess since not a lot of people believe in ghosts, one can blame any unexplainable happenings on old plumbing or the house settling.

Don't buy a house that is next to a cemetery or was once a funeral home - I had a friend from high school who lived above her father's funeral parlor which she now owns herself. Did she have ghostly experiences? Yes, and she told us amazing stories, but they were all benign in nature. There were no mean ghosts who threw things around the room. Mostly, she said the ghosts commented on their funerals and what their families made them wear.

However, I saw that movie *A Haunting in Connecticut* and its television version on the Discovery Channel. A twitter acquaintance, who wrote the book for this paranormal story, has said publicly that this entire episode was a hoax, Even with this information, I have to believe it is still best not to live in an old funeral home. Okay, let me amend that. It's okay to live in an old funeral home but unlike the people in this book, do the smart thing and remove the embalming equipment from the basement before you make it a bedroom for your young sons, and here is another tip: don't use the freezer that once housed the cadavers as a place to store your groceries. Get a new freezer. Life will be much easier.

Stressed Out? Not When I Have my Hedge Clippers

This was a week of stress. I admit that I did it to myself. I started to think about work stuff and family stuff and then I couldn't sleep, and then I got more stressed because I was tired and well, you know how that vicious circle goes.

I tried to de-stress with running and yoga, but still the stress and insomnia remained until last night. What did I do differently? I took out my electric hedge clippers.

I know what you are thinking… "Uh oh, Should I be afraid?" Well, the answer is: Yes, you should. Nothing good can come out of a situation that involves a stressed out, and most likely, perimenopausal woman who has in her possession electric hedge clippers.

I love my hedge trimmers. They make a lot of bad things go away. This is how it works. First, I get out my two, 100-foot extension cords. Then, I survey the front and backyards to see which bushes and trees need trimming. Depending upon the severity of my stress, I can chop off one branch of a shrub or every freaking leaf that dwells on my humble parcel of land. This was a day when I knew branches would be shaking with fear.

I started out with the idea that I would just trim and shape things up. This was the first trim of the spring, and the trees and bushes were about to enjoy their first haircut of the season in the hands of a sleep-deprived maniac. I began in the front yard, where these red thorny bushes grow. I hate these bushes whether I am in a peaceful mood or an agitated state of mind. The people who owned the house before us planted them to keep people and dogs off the lawn. Yes, they were welcoming souls. Unfortunately, the thorns from these bushes wind up everywhere. If I walk out to the mailbox without shoes, I get thorns in my feet. If I park my car too close to them and have to squeeze myself through them, I get scratched, and I bleed. These bushes were first on the decapitation—oops, I mean trimming list.

So, I took my blades to them. I was like a ninja warrior waving my sword in the air mentally envisioning where I would deliver my first blow. I was in that blissful chopping, trimming and thinning zone. I was focused. After the thorn bushes, I moved on to the boxwoods and then these piney-thing bushes I have yet to identify. I even found a stray poison ivy vine growing and I took that out too.

"Begone, toxic weed!" I laughed aloud with a confident cockiness I had not felt in a long time. "You will not give me hives this year!"

Well, to be truthful, the jury is still out on the whole hives thing. I did brush against the poison ivy before I whacked it, and I do get severe reactions, so if I have no new humor out in the next few weeks, you can pretty much assume anaphylactic shock got me.

After the front, I hit the backyard trees and shrubs. It was nothing short of nirvana. I could feel the stress leaving my body each time the clippers hit an unruly branch. It was only when I sliced through the overgrown forsythias that I noticed how relaxed I had become. In fact, I realized I was singing. Everything seemed to be at peace with the world again. I was happy; the birds were chirping. I guess they could have been chirping out of fright. I can't be sure, but I might have made a few of my feathered friends homeless in my quest for neater shrubbery. When I was done, I walked around my property to inspect my work. My house looked superb from the outside and now with the shrubbery so much shorter and thinner, I knew more sunlight could stream into my windows. I was excited.

Proud of what I had accomplished and now feeling so much more like myself, I poured myself a light drink and sat down on my back porch to admire my work. My husband came home about a half hour later after umpiring a baseball game. Apparently, he noticed the neatly trimmed bushes right away.

"Bad day?" He queried.

"Why do you ask?" I answered.

"We have no landscaping left!"

"It will grow back."

That was all that was said about the shrubbery that night. My husband has learned that when my stress and estrogen levels collide, it is best that he neither ask too many questions nor get too close to me and my friend, the electric hedge clippers.

A Day in the Life of a Chocolate Frosting Addict

Well, it's happened again. I gave into my temptation. It is my own fault. I baked the cake, and I insisted on using two different colored frostings – yes, they were Betty Crocker canned frostings, but they are my favorite. There was a lot of chocolate left over, and it didn't seem right to let it go to waste. I thought about the starving children in the third world who would love to eat my chocolate frosting. I also wondered if the starving children in the first and second world would like my frosting too. Where exactly are the first and second worlds? Anyway, to be honest, it's not that I would give any of them my frosting. I am pretty protective over my frosting. I would give them real food, and I am assuming my donations to the Red Cross go for exactly that. I would be a little disappointed if they took my pledge and turned it into chocolate frosting.

Anyway, I had a bad day. I was trying to write an article, and my "star" of the article would not cooperate. Not only was she ticked off that she had to be interviewed, but she made it clear that she was a better writer than me. After all, she took a creative writing class at the community college annex, and the teacher told her she was dripping with talent. Yes, "dripping" was the word she used.

I let her words go in one ear and out the other, but then she said the strangest thing. She said she was so sure of her writing ability that she wanted to edit the article that I was writing about her. I almost spit out my coffee. But I told her politely,

"You will have to take that up with my editor."

To which she said,

"What would your editor know?"

To which I said,

"I think plenty. That is why she is an editor."

Then, in a very sweet voice, I said a mean thing: I asked the writing phenom where she was published.

"I write for my church bulletin," she answered. To which I had to respond,

"The church bulletin--even if it's the freaking Vatican--is not considered being published, and you should keep your day job."

I probably shouldn't have said that directly to her, but she had it coming. It did shut her up, and I did finish the interview, but then I had to relay what I said to my editor who laughed uncontrollably and then admitted we might have to pay for that remark. I said, "I know, but really--the church bulletin?" She laughed again, and we made plans to meet for drinks in two weeks.

Oh, yes, the chocolate frosting--I'm getting there. All the aggravation from the wannabe writer chick triggered my need to eat the leftover chocolate frosting. As I was spooning it out of the can, a sense of calm and euphoria came over me. The day took on an entirely new spin. I felt empowered, satisfied and to be honest, a bit buzzed. I guess all the sugar finally hit me about halfway through the can.

I took advantage of the sugar high and completed research for two more articles and then mowed my lawn. My only worry about my chocolate frosting habit is that the government will find out about the buzz factor and want to label it as some kind of mood-enhancing drug and force me to go to rehab with Lindsay Lohan. Just in case this happens, I have been hoarding my frosting. I have multiple flavors hidden in my pantry. Yes, it's true. While some people keep emergency survival kits filled with bandages, water and beans, I keep frosting. When you think about it, I would be a lot more pleasant in the post-apocalyptic world than the person who only ingests beans.

Anyway, I have to go do an interview for another article. But I am prepared. I have my coffee and a can of frosting on my desk. That should get me through the day until I go to gym and oh yeah, my root canal. In the words of my dentist: "Frosting? You eat frosting? This root canal you do deserve."

Computer eHarmony?

I rarely use my printer. I keep all my work on my computer, and I back it up in some way. However, I do have one editor who sends such specific instructions for articles that I feel the need to print them out and keep them in front of me when I am working on her assignments.

Last week, she emailed me one of her usual assignments that included about 30 points she wanted me to cover. So, I saved the file and hit print. I waited a few minutes, but nothing happened. I went over to my printer to take a closer look. I could see the green light, so I knew the printer was on. There was paper in the tray, and nothing seemed to be wrong. The printer was just not responding.

I have a new laptop, so I thought that I forgot to set up my printer with the new computer. I went into control panel to confirm that I had linked it to my laptop correctly. Sure enough, my printer was listed as the default printer. It even had that little green check mark next to it to show me it was indeed the printer of record.

In years past, I would have called my husband, the engineer, to talk me through these technology glitches. But I have been trying to be more self-sufficient when it comes to my computer. Besides, he never answers his office phone anyway. He says it's the new phone system or he is in the lab out of reach; I think he avoids me.

In his defense, I will admit that when technology issues have arisen in the past, I might not have been the most calm and receptive person when it comes to fixing the problem. He wants to give me long, drawn out solutions that require a 10,000-step procedure to make my computer do what I want it to do. I want to press one key and abracadabra, it's fixed. And if he can't give me that one key to press, I might get a teeny bit snippy.

I was totally perplexed and wondering why I could not get the printer to print, so I decided to do the old rebooting trick. I first rebooted the desktop computer that is command central for the rest of the computers and the printer in my home network. After that computer had restarted properly, I hit print again. I got a message that said,

"Directories are not active and cannot be accessed." I didn't like that message. So, I ignored it, emitted a string of expletives, and went on to my step two: rebooting my laptop.

I could feel my anxiety level rising a bit because, to be honest, the rebooting thing is the only technical fix I know for computers. If it did not work, I knew I was screwed. When my computer had completed the reboot, I held my breath and hit "print" again. This time, I got a message that said:

"Computer does not recognize printer."

"What the hell does that mean?" I screamed. "The printer is listed as the default printer. Both computers are up and running, and my computer does not recognize the printer? Is it kidding me?"

So, I tried to figure out a way for them to recognize each other. Out of desperation, I took my laptop over to the printer and said,

"Printer, meet my laptop! Laptop, meet my printer!"

I gave them a minute to get acquainted. I even put on the little webcam thing so they could have a picture of each other. Then, I took my laptop back to my desk and hit "print" again. Guess what? It worked. I kid you not. Out of the printer came my editor's instructions. I was amazed. When I saw what my little matchmaking attempt had done, I thought I should dim the lights, give my laptop and printer a bottle of wine and let technology love take its course.

I was so impressed with my non-conventional solution that I called my husband to brag. I left a voice mail explaining how the computer and printer seemed to have an emotional moment. Within a minute, he called back. Yeah, within a minute--he definitely avoids me. He said that it was impossible for the printer and laptop to have that kind of connection, and I must have done something to fix the issue. I accused him of being unromantic and thinking too much with the left side of his brain. He asked if I had been drinking.

Anyway, whatever I did to the computer and laptop did the trick. My printer has spit out everything I have asked it to spit out since that day. Maybe I did press something unintentionally, and it was the right key to hit. Maybe the rebooting had a delayed reaction and the printer was set to go with the next command. Or maybe – just maybe, even computers need a little romance to get back on track.

Mob Wives: Not Ladies One Invites to Tea

I tuned into a reality show called *Mob Wives*. Presented by VH1, this entertainment gem focuses on women of Staten Island, New York who are married to gangsters.

I was confused right from the start. First, how come they are bragging about being married to mobsters on national TV? I thought one had to keep a low profile or not admit they are in any way connected to this lifestyle. What happened to discretion and being worried about the embarrassment that comes from people knowing you are married to a violent criminal?

These loud women held nothing back when it came to their husbands who are either behind bars or ex-guests of the penal system who became guests because the feds would not stop harassing them. Yes, apparently, murder, loan sharking and drug trafficking should not be reasons for imprisonment since their husbands were only trying to provide for their families and put food on the table.

How did reality for these women become so skewed? In the episode I watched, one of the wives was upset because her best friend, who is also married to a gangster, threw herself a birthday bash and invited another woman whose gangster father turned state's evidence. The upset friend believed that the snitch's daughter should be ostracized from their circle of friends because of her father's big mouth which led to many of her family getting sent to the big house. Got it? To be honest, the upset chick did not use the word ostracize. She sort of used the F-word to get her point across. The birthday hostess disagreed as did another one of the women attending the party and a shoving match complete with a vulgar verbal exchange commenced.

Let me take this moment to interject something here: First, I am not unfamiliar with the F-word and it does flow from my mouth on occasion, but these women took swearing to an entirely new level. VH1 had one continuous censor bleep going for about five minutes. Second: I am originally from NYC and I do have relatives who live in Staten Island and none of them behave this way. They are normal, hard-working people who find crime repulsive. I just thought I should throw this in so people understand that while Staten Island obviously has its mob element, it's not all about that – I don't think.

Okay, back to the show. So, the one doing the shoving is this buff mob wife who spends hours in the gym hitting a punching bag. There was also a subplot in this episode. You are shocked, right? I was. I didn't think these women could be deep enough to have a subplot, but I was mistaken.

The subplot was deeply moving. Apparently, the mob husbands call home from prison to help their kids do their homework. I am not making this stuff up. One of the wives refuses to tell her kids that their father is in prison, and she tells him he is calling from another country where he has to work. Okay, does she not understand the concept of being on a reality TV show? Perhaps she didn't read the contract that stated her business would be broadcast all over the world including details about her husband's imprisonment. My guess is that after this episode aired, her kid found out in school the next day that his dad is not serving his country overseas but rather serving 20-to-life in a prison in another state.

In Search of a New Personality

Many people tell me that they know exactly the type of person I am. They say there is no hidden mystery or dark side to my personality that has yet to be discovered. This sort of upsets me. I would like to be mysterious to some extent. I don't want to be an open book that bores people after a few chapters. I want to have a hidden side; I want to have depth; and dammit, I am going to get some.

So, to start me on my way to becoming a more intriguing individual, I have decided to adopt an alter ego. Hey, many writers do this. I know writers who can float in and out of their alter egos without so much as batting an eyelash. The world may think they are tortured souls when reading their words, but away from the computer, their most tortured experience is being a night manager of the local 7-11 or Dunkin Donuts. If these writers can capture the imagination of their readers, I can too! Well, maybe capturing people's imaginations might be too much to ask. How about if I just get an alternate personality that makes people wonder if I have to take medication on a daily basis or if it is an on-again, off-again thing depending on my moods.

In keeping with this new quest of adding dimension to my personality, I have come up with several possibilities for my alter ego. These are not cast in stone, so if anyone has other alter ego suggestions that they think might serve me better, feel free to let me know.

Harry Putter (the next best thing to Harry Potter): I don't have to be the real Harry Potter – just a pseudo Harry Potter. I would want to be cute and speak with a British accent. I would also want to be able to fly around on a broomstick because that is so environmentally correct, and, of course, I would want the power to change people who annoy me into rodents or inanimate objects. I think as Harry Putter, I could solve the entire road rage epidemic that exists in this country. Yes, anyone who cuts me off or switches lanes without using a turn signal gets zapped and turned into a poor bug that goes splat on my windshield. See, I can be dark. I think this alter ego would be spectacular at horror fiction.

Alberta Einstein (Rocket Scientist): I hear the giggles of doubt already. But let me just say that I took AP Physics in high school. Yeah, I bet that surprised a bunch of you. Okay, ceramics was closed and I needed an elective and I thought "How hard can this be?" It was really hard, but I passed. Granted, I never begged so much in my life for a D, but I passed. So, I think that I can pull off a rocket scientist alter ego. I would not have to be someone on the Stephen Hawking level. I see my alter ego as a run-of-the-mill, NASA, female scientist who toils endlessly in the lab trying to find ways to make the dried food experience in space more appealing for the astronauts. I would think that a lab rat of this stature could have a truly dark side to her personality, and I can see her writing some intense science fiction.

Lola Fallōva (Exotic Dancer): This personality would represent the darkest of sides, but on a positive note, I would probably have a lot of extra dollar bills to spend on fun things. No one is more tortured or misunderstood than the exotic dancer who is forced into this life due to some heartbreaking tragedy that was not of her making. Okay, some just like to strip for the money, but they are probably still tortured. Anyway, I can see Lola writing a lot of erotic fiction. I bet she has the stories and the vocabulary to win her an adult fiction award or two.

Alice Brady (live-in housekeeper): This character even comes with theme music. Sing to the tune of the "Brady Bunch". *Here's the story - of Alice Brady - who was living with a blended family. There were six kids plus dopey parents, but Alice is the true Mystery.* I'm sorry; I think this alter ego got carried away. Anyway, Alice has to be tortured. She cleans up after all those kids while the husband and wife put on shows in the backyard and pretend to have sex. What does Alice have? Nothing - except a small cramped room off the kitchen. I would be tortured and bitter in this situation too. So, I think Alice could write cooking/murder mystery novels where all the victims are killed in the gourmet kitchens of celebrity homes.

Well, those are all the alter egos I could come up with right now. Feel free to suggest any others to me. I will keep an open mind. Rest assured, one day, I will come up with the perfect "other personality" that might shock the hell out of the writing world. Or maybe, I already own a dark, alternate personality, and readers just do not recognize my other half. Yes, maybe I have become my alter ego. Happy reading!

The Magic Shopping Machine

With my daughter living at home again, we have re-connected on one of our favorite activities: shopping. I have to admit that during her college years, I didn't go to the mall nearly as much because no one was around to lend a helping hand with my wardrobe choices. However, last week, as I was getting ready to run an errand, my daughter gave me the up-and-down once over and said,

"Mom, those jeans are so big on you. You can fit two of you in there."

While usually a comment like this would send me skipping off to Friendly's for ice cream, I just laughed and invited her to go shopping with me.

She eagerly consented, and with a new clothes goal in mind, we headed to the King of Prussia mall or what we call, The Mother Ship. As we were walking near the food court, this nice-looking man jumped in front of us and asked me in a very excited voice,

"What size do you wear?"

I admit my first reaction was to let him have it in the stomach. Luckily for him, he reads faces well and put up his hands in a protective stance before I had a chance to land the first punch. Then he blurted out,

"I'm not trying to harass you, I swear! I want to tell you about our size-scanning machine that can tell you exactly what size clothing you should be buying and where you can find that clothing in the mall."

Okay, I was a little intrigued. So, he brought us over to this metal capsule contraption and showed us how it would work. First, I would remove my shoes, and then place all metals such as keys, jewelry, cell phone, coins and belts on the safety shelves inside the scanner. Then, as I stood inside the machine, I would need to hold still while the low-power radio waves bounced off my skin. The waves would then transfer the data of my personal size information to a barcoded ticket. After the scanning was complete, I would insert my ticket at a kiosk next to the scanner and type in an item of clothing I was interested in buying. And like magic, I would be directed to a store and the exact merchandise that was guaranteed to fit me.

Well, I have to say that while it sounded like a good idea, I had reservations. First off, I had to wonder who invented this machine. I can picture some reject from the Department of Homeland Security or the FAA coming up with this gadget. Not to be too cynical, but I've had similar experiences going through airport security — or worse, my mammogram.

The second reservation I had about this scanner is that it takes away the unknown. A scanning would save me the trouble of taking 15 items of all different sizes into the dressing room. Scanning would take the guesswork out of what size clothing I should try on. But that guesswork allows me to live in denial. I have said it before: I think denial is highly underrated. I embrace denial. If I step into this Star Trek time machine-looking contraption, the denial is gone. I don't think I can cope if this high-tech personal shopper informs me that my ideal size is three sizes larger than what I think it is.

And my last problem with the size-scanning device is that it is located right across from the dessert crepes kiosk. Who the hell was the genius who picked this spot in the mall? If I go and get scanned and find out I'm larger than I thought I was, I am not going to shake it off. No, I am going to lapse into a depressed state and walk over to the dessert kiosk and get one of their banana and vanilla ice cream-filled crepes with chocolate sauce and whipped cream. Would this make the scanner people happy? I would think not unless, they own the crepe kiosk too.

After the scanner man finished his presentation, he asked me if I was ready to take the step into the machine that would change my life. I thought he was getting a little cocky. If I walked into that machine and it erased all traces of cellulite or straightened my hair, then I would announce to the world that this was a machine that has changed my life.

Anyway, very politely – well, sort of – I told the scanning man I was not interested and gave him back his brochure, and my daughter and I went about our business. To be honest, we headed to the crepe kiosk because it smelled so good while we were listening to the scanning lecture, and we couldn't resist. After we split the crepe, we decided to skip the new pair of jeans because I felt too bloated to try anything on. See, now if that scanner could zap bloat, then I would shout from the top of the mall escalator that it is truly a life-changing machine.

Should I Star in a Workout Video

I work out a great deal. I used to swim all the time, but I felt as if I needed to change up my routine a bit and surprise my muscles. I think they got used to "what was coming" and decided they didn't need to work as hard to get toned. So, for the past few months, instead of diving into the pool, I head to the treadmill, elliptical and weights.

The most difficult aspect of switching to "dry" workouts has been learning what to wear at the gym. When I swim, I wear my Speedo one-piece suit underneath old sweatpants and a comfy sweatshirt that is about three sizes too big. I don't have to look good to walk through the gym. My swimming cover up clothing is there to keep me warm while I dash from the parking lot to the pool and back to the parking lot again. The nice thing also about swimming is that once I get to the pool, I am in full disguise. No one cares what I look like or even if they did, they could not tell who I am. The swim cap completely covers my big hair (yes, I did have to get the super duper model), and it is impossible to determine who is swimming the laps behind my purple goggles.

However, now that I exercise among the masses, the entire situation has changed. I am on center stage with every other sweaty workout person on the planet, and I have to say, I don't think I am a pretty sight. So, I have to wonder why my fitness center, which is part of a national chain, sent me an email inviting me to participate in a video profiling me and my workout routine. Yes, they want me to be in a video to show people how wonderful it is to workout at my gym, and how the experience has enriched my life.

I have to guess that the sole purpose of this company's PR department is to sink the entire chain. Why else are they inviting me into this promotion? According to the email, they sought me out because I am a very active member of my gym. Did they even bother to see what I looked like before they invited me to do the video? Perhaps, they should have checked my membership photo. They took that beauty about 6 AM on a rainy day – not a flattering pose.

If I had to do this video, I guess I could don makeup for the cause. Usually, I don't believe in makeup for the gym. However, I refuse to take the time to do my hair. I admit that I do wet it down before I do my workout regimen because I don't want to scare anyone, but once I start exercising, the curls just boing back into place and the bulk of my tresses expand in direct proportion to my increasing speed on the treadmill. Last week, an Asian lady with straight, silky black hair commented that my treadmill should record not only my heart rate and the miles I run but also how much my hair grows during a workout. She thought she was being cute and funny. I was tempted to hit the "stop" button on her treadmill and watch as she catapulted across the gym. I figured a sudden stop would send her flying pretty far since she only weighed about 87 pounds sweaty.

Next challenge for this video: my workout clothes. Okay, I did get a few pairs of the new cute yoga pants for my gym workout and some tee shirts. But I don't have the tight fitting stuff that many of the women wear. I don't have the coordinating gym ensembles that include the Capri pants, matching sports bra and tank tops, sweat bands, head bands and iPod arm bands. I have the little iPod that doesn't require an armband, and I only got it recently. Before this leap into technology, I would sing to myself on the treadmill. Sometimes, if there was a really gross sweaty man running next to me, I sang loudly so he would think I was crazy and that would prompt him to move to a new machine.

Anyway, after I read the email, I sent the marketing people at the corporate headquarters of my fitness center a nice note. I thanked them for thinking of me and I was happy they were happy with my commitment to exercise, but I turned down the video gig. I told them exactly what I told all of you, and they too agreed that maybe I would not be the best person for a video which is meant to extol the benefits of working out at one of their clubs. I also said that if they ever want to do a swimming video and they could assure me that only my head and neck would be shown and I could appear in my swim cap and goggles disguise, I would be on board. They will let me know on that. In the meantime, I gave them the name of the cute Asian lady who runs next to me. They are going to call her. Let's face it: nothing sells gym memberships like petite women who never had an ounce of fat on them in their entire lives.

The Speeding Ticket Gender Gap

A study by the auto insurance industry reveals that women stand a better chance of getting out of a traffic ticket than men. Gee, what a surprise. I don't mean to be facetious, but the auto industry spent God knows how many thousands of dollars figuring this out? And for those who think that it is only young women who reap the benefits of getting off with just a warning, think again. While it is true that 33 percent of younger women can talk themselves out of a ticket, the percentages of women not getting tickets does not go down significantly until a woman reaches the age of 75.

In looking back on my driving experience, I have to admit that I would agree with this study's findings. Allow me to take you through my police officer encounters. For the record, I maintain that I was the victim of a speed trap in both of these occurrences and only once did I ever have to pay a fine. And that was because my husband was sitting next to me in the car, and I couldn't do "my best" to get out of the ticket.

The first speeding incident happened on I-81 in the Lackawanna County, Pennsylvania. I was traveling to my in-laws for Thanksgiving. It was late, and I didn't think I was going that fast on the deserted road. As I coasted down this pretty big hill on the highway, I noticed flashing lights behind me. I wanted to race the cop to the New York border, but my goody-two-shoes husband insisted we pull over. Anyway, at first, the police officer was just going to lecture me. I pleaded ignorance, and he believed me, but then he caught sight of another person in my passenger seat. He pointed his flashlight on my husband's face, and that is when my opportunity to escape fine free vanished. It was funny how the officer's demeanor changed immediately. Before I had a chance to cry the words "speed trap", the officer had written me up for going 20 miles over the speed limit which resulted in a $300 fine. However, the officer said that if I didn't fight the ticket, there would be no points. It wasn't a horrible result, but I guess I do not have to tell you that I was not so grateful that Thanksgiving.

The next time I was pulled over was about five years later. I was coming home from the newspaper where I worked as a reporter. It was 3 AM, and I was going a little faster than the 25 mile-per-hour speed limit through a not-so-nice part of town. In my rearview mirror, I saw an unmarked car pull up with his lights flashing. The officer didn't even get out of the car at first. He waited for a second patrol car to pull up behind him.

"Great!" I thought. "Who's coming next -- the freaking SWAT team?" The two officers got out of their cars and started to chat. Finally, the guy in the unmarked car came over and when he saw that I was alone, his entire attitude softened. He also could see that I was a little ticked off.

"Why are you out so late by yourself?" was his first question.

"I'm a reporter, and I just finished my shift. Are you thinking about giving me a ticket? I asked in my most aggravated tone. "How fast could I have been going that you needed to pull me over in an unmarked vehicle at three in the morning? Are you bored tonight? No criminals to catch?"

He very quietly asked for my license and then he added, "Are you just going to yell at me through this whole thing? Can't we just be friends? I would let you go but I already started to write the ticket. That other guy is my supervisor, and I can't rip it up."

"Yeah, yeah, yeah," I responded impatiently.

"Well, do you want to know how fast you were going?"

"Officer, it is very late. I was taking extra care to watch the road, not my speedometer." (I can't take credit for this line. I heard my mother use it on several occasions, and it always worked well for her. I have passed it on to my daughter as well.)

"Wow, good one!" he said approvingly. "For that comeback, I'll meet you at court and tell the judge it was my fault. I will make sure you don't get a fine or anything. I feel bad I pulled you over."

With the promise that my driving record would remain squeaky clean, I forgave the officer. The next week, I was ducking behind my car while covering a hostage situation, and I saw my officer and his supervisor. They were busy pointing their guns and all, but they waved. So after the armed suspect gave himself up, I walked up to both of them to say hello and to remind my officer of his promise to get me out of the traffic ticket. He assured me he remembered. On the day of my hearing, he showed up and defended me, and the judge literally erased the ticket from my driving record.

This officer turned out to be a good egg. As for my husband, he just kept harping on the fact that I got stopped for a ticket. I kept reminding him that I was not convicted of that traffic violation. But he kept going on and on and on until he came home one day foaming at the mouth. He was stopped for speeding and got a ticket. Did I make fun? Oh yeah, I was insufferable. But, I did pull it together to be a good wife for his court date. Not only did I show up with him at court, but I brought our daughter as well dressed in the cutest little outfit she owned. The judge took one look at his devoted family and tossed that ticket, and then told my husband to take us both out to dinner.

If I think about it, I kind of like the idea that women get out of tickets more often than men. I know that sounds sexist, but I think it keeps the power between the sexes a bit more balanced, plus I think when the police show a more sensitive side, people might respect the law more. I know I do.

Learning to Read my Pets' Minds

On a daily basis, my email box is filled with offers from schools that want to help me change my life. I can go back to school and earn all kinds of credentials. I can get a graduate or law degree that will be worth nothing because it is from an internet school no one has heard of. I can learn to become a chef, a makeup artist to the stars, or even a psychic. I mention the psychic one because when I saw this offer, I could not resist and clicked the "send me more information" button which led me to a free, four-part "Develop your Psychic Skills" class.

Not being a psychic yet, I did not foresee that enrolling in this freebie series would put me on every new age mailing list known to the cosmos. Granted, I love new age stuff – the wackier the better, but since clicking the "become-all-knowing" button, I have been asked to look into a lot of strange things. I got an invitation to learn a new meditation technique that will catapult me across time and space, which by the way, sounds like a hell of a lot of fun. I was asked to enroll in a class that would teach me how to chant my way to financial freedom. Chanting will prove to be challenging because I cannot carry a tune. I would think that if I cannot sing, I will not be good at chanting. However, on a positive note, if I chant, people might throw money at me if I promise to just shut up.

Anyway, as I was perusing my email, I had this gut feeling that another exciting learning experience was waiting to be discovered (See, the free psychic classes are already paying off). As I glanced at the 230 unopened emails, there was my invitation to become an intuitive animal communicator.

Hey, this isn't just about being a Dog Whisperer! No, if I take this course and make my two easy payments of $149.50, I can learn to hear what my dogs are actually thinking. And it's not just dogs. I will be able to read the minds of cats, ducks, ferrets, horses, birds, lions, tigers, bears and even goldfish. I have often wondered what goes on in the mind of a goldfish. Are they happy flitting around their bowls, or do they get bored with their limited surroundings?

Well, as it turns out, I may not have to wonder about this much longer. I can sign up today and learn to be an animal psychic. The best part is that I do not have to commute to the psychic campus. No, I can take all my classes in the privacy of own home. Yes, my mind can absorb the psychic signals while I sit in my pajamas and listen to the course via telephone or internet. It's like the University of Phoenix meets Harry Potter's Hogwarts. This is so cool! And guess what else? When I am done with my course, the ad says that people will come knocking on my door to pay me for my expertise.

How great is this? No longer will I need to send out query letters to editors begging them to read my stuff. No, I will possess such strong psychic powers that clients will seek me out! I am now ready to throw my writing career away for the lucrative and selfless profession known as the animal psychic. It's like I have had a life-transforming moment – an epiphany if you will.

I showed this course to my husband and daughter, both of whom looked at me as if I had definitely crossed over the sanity line.

"You want to take what course?" my husband asked. "We already know what the dogs are thinking. They are not that hard to figure out. Eat, poop, walk, sleep – we already have their buzzwords down."

"But now, I can tell you when they are depressed or have had their feelings hurt or if they have emotional issues from their birth," I countered.

"They were strays; of course they have issues," he argued. They lived on the streets before they found you, the sap of all saps. They are happy now. Why make them relive that pain? "

Okay, up until the last part of that conversation, I thought he was taking me seriously. Apparently not. Anyway, I sent a "NO" back to the animal psychic course invitation explaining that it was too expensive for me to take on right now. I guess if they were truly a legit school, they would offer some kind of grant or scholarship program, but there was nothing. So, I told my dogs that I wouldn't be reading their minds, and they did not react much, so I guess they are okay with that. I would know for sure if they were okay if I took the course, but that ship has now sailed.

The disappointment over not becoming an animal psychic will wane soon. As we speak there are at least 10 new emails awaiting my attention. And guess what? There is one that is daring me to be a ghost hunter. Now, we're cooking.

Hot Wax and Hurt Feelings Do Not Mix

Believe it or not, sometimes I get into quiet moods when I do not like to talk. I know; it is hard to believe However, every once in a while it happens. For me, quiet is not a sign of depression or the blues. Usually, I grow quiet because I am tired or in a place where I have a true fear about expressing my opinions. I know that sounds cowardly, but there are times when I opt to bite my tongue to avoid pain, disfigurement or possible death. Recently, I had one of those days.

I started writing at 6 AM to get a jump on my work. I was sweating a writing deadline that was looming, and I was still in need of two interview sources. By the time noon rolled around, I was done in. I decided to take a break from the computer and head to the salon to get my eyebrows waxed. You might think that this is an odd choice for a computer break, but, honestly, I had let too much time lapse since the last skin-ripping adventure. It's not that I was sporting a uni-brow, but I was definitely getting a bit self-conscious walking around in public.

Anyway, my wax specialist, Kim, was chatting non-stop as she was preparing to spoon the hot wax on my eyelids. She was asking me questions, but I was giving her one-word answers, and it must have bugged her because she said,

"Are you mad at me?"

"No! Why would you ask that?" I responded with a genuine alarmed tone in my voice.

"You are so quiet today. You have not said anything about my new hair cut or asked about my baby or the salon."

Wow, she felt neglected, and this was my fault. I guess she was used to me being interested in her life, and yesterday, she thought I was not interested, so I hurt her feelings. Trust me when I say the last person you want to piss off or hurt is the person who is pouring hot wax on any part of your body. The hot wax is not even the issue. It's the ripping-off-the-hair-from-your-body-parts that become the issue if the person doing the ripping is feeling a sense of anger toward you.

"I am so sorry, please forgive me!" I begged aloud. "I am just tired; I swear! How is your son? Getting ready for pre-school?"

Those words seemed to relax Kim a bit, and the rest of the waxing session went without a hitch. After she tamed my brows, I paid my bill and left her a healthy tip just to make sure there were no hard feelings. As I drove off, I thought about the close call I had with her, and I also realized that I do go out of my way to be extra nice, attentive and non-argumentative to the people who possess the potential to hurt me or my wallet. This revelation inspired me to create my "Never Piss Off" list:

Kim - my hot wax person is obviously first one on the list. With Kim, eyebrows are the least of my worries. I can always draw on new eyebrows with a pencil if she gets testy. It's the bikini wax that might cause me more pain than I am willing to deal with. I already find bikini waxing embarrassing and loathsome, but it is sort of a necessity especially during the summer months. Sometimes, when Kim is in a talkative mood, she starts opining on the situation in South Korea. I think it is South Korea, but I can't be sure because she starts talking in her native tongue, and she loses me. She also becomes quite animated, and the wax flies around and I do not want to insult her, so I distract her with questions about her baby and business to keep her calm.

My dentist - My dentist listens to political shows on the radio while he is working on me. I would prefer Mozart or something more tranquil, but he is the one holding the drill, so I let him be. If you asked my dentist what my political views are, he would say that they would mirror his exactly. I probably agree with maybe one-tenth of his political views, but while I am in that chair, I am his biggest supporter. Let's face it: I am the definition of a captive audience with him, so I will temporarily adopt any political credo if it means I never have to hear the words "Root Canal", "Periodontal surgery" or "Extraction".

My gynecologist - I do not think I need to go into specifics here. You might be eating lunch. Let's just say that my pap smear is not the time to have heated discussions on religion, global affairs, the AMA lobby, or – and I cannot stress this one enough, health care reform.

The servers in any restaurant: Piss off a waiter or waitress and you will definitely get invisible foreign matter in your food. You will never be able to prove it, but if have cramps or diarrhea two days after you had an altercation with a server or bus person, the chances are high you are paying the price for that altercation.

Well, this is my short list. I know I have neglected to mention others who impact my life on a daily basis, and if you are one of my service providers, who I have forgotten, please do not get insulted or take it out on me next time I come in for an appointment. Believe me, there is always room to write about you later.

My Take on Social Media

Social media to me is an amazing phenomenon. I admit when it first arrived on the scene, I thought it was a fad that would fade. I never thought people could have meaningful connections via the internet. I am going to say right now that I was 100 percent wrong. If there is anyone who has had a complete change of mind on the concept of social media, it is me.

Two years ago, I entered the world of Facebook for two reasons: the first was that my husband and I started an NFL analysis site. A publicist friend of mine told me to think about giving Facebook a whirl for promotion. The second reason I went on Facebook was because my dogs' godmother signed up. Yes, my dogs have a godmother in case I die or become incapacitated and cannot handle their daily canine needs. I feel better knowing the girls are in good hands.

"Who will want to be my friend on Facebook besides you?" I asked Godmother Beth.

"You don't need tons of friends; people find you," she assured me.

"I don't have a good picture. I won't have to do one of those pucker-lip poses like the young chicks, do I? Pursed lips on them look sexy, but I would like a fish gasping for its last breath."

"People put up any picture. It doesn't matter. No one is going to judge you."

Apparently, she had not seen recent photos of me. Despite my nervousness over the photo, I signed up. Within days, college friends who I had not heard from since graduation "pinged" me and asked to be friends. They chatted about our old dorm mates and old boyfriends. They sent me pictures of their most recent spouses and their kids. Yeah, it's a regular old reunion.

When I told my publicist friend that I joined Facebook, she squealed with excitement and insisted I try out a few less known social media sites that she was helping to promote. As it turned out, these sites were not the top tier of social networking. I tried to be polite and request and accept friends, but most of the people on those sites wanted me to join their multi-level marketing companies with promises that I could be a millionaire in about six months. If it was that easy to be a millionaire in six months, how come there are not more millionaires around? The other invitations I got seemed to revolve around religion or spirituality. I don't begrudge anyone their beliefs, but I am just not a person who can commit to a religion easily especially one that wants me to abandon this planet of sin for a new life on Venus. I know Earth has its problems, but I am still sort of fond of it, and I don't feel the urgency to leave it just yet. I no longer interact with anyone on those sites.

Once I started to feel a little more comfortable about Facebook, I took another brave step into Twitter which was also on the advice of my publicist friend. Well, to be honest, she threw me into Twitter. She started a new account for me and started posting my work on various writing sites.

I guess I understand why people pay her. She is tireless in her goal for promotion, and she gets the job done. She says I have a deep-seeded hang up about self-promotion; she thinks it's too much Catholic school. I think she may be right. Anyway, the dive into social media has been nothing short of enlightening.

Twitter and the writing sites are my favorite social media tools. These sites are to new contacts what Facebook is to old contacts. The people I have met on these sites have proven to be good friends. We not only converse online, but we talk on the phone, and several I have met in person. I have made friends from all over the world, and may I just say how much I appreciate the fact that the rest of the world learns the English language. I try to converse in Italian and Spanish with some of my international friends, but I know my skills are woeful at best. However, my friends from across the sea never make fun of me unless I accidentally call them a bad name.

I do get nervous about social media too. There are always news reports about computer viruses coming from Facebook applications, and I worry that the Federal Government may interpret some of my Tweets as threats to Homeland Security. I read that they monitor tweets. I don't know if that's true, but it is a little unnerving. I did get a spamming virus one time on Twitter. I thought I was sending out my link to my blog, but I was sending out a link to porn. Honestly, I do not know how that happened. Many people yelled at me and unfollowed me, but one kind lady told me what was going on and walked me through the solution.

So, what have I learned? I learned that there is a world of great people out there and some not so great people. In fact, I met a guy on Twitter who offered to bring me to California so I could experience the thrill of complete and open love in his cabin. I thought he was kidding; it turned out he wasn't. Luckily, Facebook and Twitter have that un-follow and block option. It does come in handy sometimes.

I hear many people complain that social media has destroyed the need for human contact. I disagree completely. I have made more friends on social media in the past two years than I have in person in the last 10 years. Is social media a substitute for in-person relationships? No way. But it does add interest to my daily life.

The Ultimate Proposal

While perusing the online news, an interesting human interest story caught my attention. It was about a man who decided to propose to his girlfriend through a crossword puzzle. It was not any crossword puzzle. It was a crossword puzzle he created himself which contained answers that spelled out "Will you marry me?"

If that was not romantic enough, he took the crossword to the *Washington Post* and paid them to publish it on a Sunday, the day his girlfriend usually did the crossword. In the early morning hours, on that Sunday, he scoured the streets to find a store that had the early morning edition, so he could make sure his girlfriend would have the proposal puzzle in her hands.

Apparently, this guy loves his girlfriend a lot, and I am sure their love will last, but I want to check back with them in about ten years just to see if that kind of romance has continued. I was touched by this guy's level of sentiment. One does not usually find this in men. I hear the boos from the Y-chromosome people, but let me ask a question: Who of you is truly capable of romance at this level? As you were reading the story about this crossword puzzle, what were you thinking?

This guy paid to put the crossword puzzle in The Washington Post. That was so over the top.

OR

Damn! the Washington Post, did he have to buy a ring too?

OR

He better not be springing for the wedding! That should be on her.

OR

I bet he got laid - a lot for that.

Any of these thoughts sound familiar? Relax, Gentlemen, this guy is an aberration. I have heard of these men from afar, but to be honest, I have never met one up close. They are more often than not, figments of a romance writer's imagination. Then again, my standards are low. If my husband puts in a load of laundry or takes out the trash without a prompt from me, I think that I am the luckiest woman in the world. It's my own fault. If I had raised the bar, I could have some chick-flick romance fly through my door too.

Now, before the entire male sex votes to have me stoned for poking fun at your missing romance gene, let me deliver some good news. This guy, the "Crossword Lover", well...he is toast. Let me explain why. He has made it impossible to outdo that proposal. Nowhere in time, will he ever be able to live up to that proposal again. Sure, his wife will always have bragging rights to the crossword puzzle; she might even have it framed, but after a few years, she will want another gesture of his love. Let's face it; he can only go downhill in the romance department after the crossword surprise. Yes, their marriage has yet to start, and the husband-to-be has already peaked.

I know his soon-to-be-wife is saying, "No, I will always remember my proposal, and no matter what happens in life, I will keep it close to my heart--always!"

But 20 years from now when he brings her a bunch of flowers from 7-Eleven for their anniversary, she is going to say,

"I was thinking about the crossword puzzle you did for me? Can't you do something like that again?"

And he is going to look at her and say,

"Are you freaking kidding me? We have college tuitions to pay and a mortgage and you want me to spend the money on a crossword puzzle for the *Washington Post*? For God's sake, we need a new car this year."

Now, Gentlemen, this is where the unromantic guy wins out. Not having ever created a crossword puzzle or a love poem or any kind of written message that is not pre-printed on a Hallmark card, your wife or girlfriend will not expect anything over the top -- ever. You can bring home those wilted roses from the 7-Eleven, and she will be thrilled, and you might even get sex for them.

So, cheer up, Men! The "Crossword Lover" may have gained media attention and become the darling of talk shows, but his fifteen minutes of fame will end. You, on the other hand, will have a lifetime to convince your girlfriend, wife or significant other that she made the right choice when she agreed to put down roots with you. Ain't love grand?

Tips on Do-It-Yourself Funerals

Somehow, I got on a funeral list. I am not talking about a specific funeral, but trends that go on in the funeral industry. My first thought as to why I get the funeral updates was that I must have done an article on this topic, but I cannot for the life of me remember researching or writing such a piece. So, being the logical person I am, I jumped from point A to point Z and decided my husband must be investigating funerals. It's not that farfetched. When he does online research, he gives everyone my email address, so his email box doesn't get filled with spam. Somewhere along the line, my email address has become our family's clearing house for stuff they were interested in, but don't want to be contacted about. But now, I am left wondering why he is investigating funerals and should I watch what I eat when he cooks.

This latest email on this macabre topic led to an article about "Do-It-Yourself" funerals. Apparently, in these tough economic times, people are looking to cut corners wherever they can and a loved one's funeral is no exception. Why spend $8,000 to put Grandma in the ground when you can shave off half the costs if you do some of the stuff on your own. Again, this is a red flag for me with my husband. He is a human being who loves to get a good deal, so allow me to ask a favor here: If there comes a time when someone out there says, "Gee, I haven't heard from Donna in a while" would you please check my freezer? It's in the basement, down the steps, hang a left. Thanks.

Do you know it's perfectly legal to do your own funeral? It's not that long ago that people did have wakes in their homes. There were no funeral parlors. You just parked the casket next to the sofa and let the booze flow and the mourning begin. Now, for most of us, it seems a bit creepy having a dead body in the house. However, with the rising costs of such an event, the funeral industry is telling customers or soon-to-be customers that a funeral can be a shared experience.

For instance, to cut down on preparation, you can opt to wash down the deceased yourself. You can do the makeup and dress the body, etc. Now again, I don't have a problem with this, but personally, if my funeral is going the economic route, I want someone who is good at makeup. I don't want someone who has held a grudge toward me or my family applying lipstick or a curling iron to my body.

You might be asking who would want to prepare their own loved one's body. Well, would you be surprised to learn that if you are a "green" person, opting to prepare the body and foregoing embalming is helping out Mother Earth? Yep, embalming chemicals and whatever else they do in funeral parlors in not a "green" procedure, so a do-it-yourself job eliminates chemical waste and the deceased becomes great mulch along the way. I could see my husband liking the mulch idea and planting me in the vegetable garden. Okay – new thought. If I'm not in the freezer, go to the garden. It's at the end of the backyard by the fence.

There are a few caveats with the whole body-in-the-house thing. First, most states have a limit on how long you can keep a dead body in your residence. Secondly, funeral professionals suggest that even if your event is taking place in the midst of a blizzard, you need to crank up the air conditioning or have a lot of dry ice on hand. When you do plan a "home" funeral, know that you can ask a funeral parlor for help in different ways. Apparently, most do offer a-la-cart services now. For instance, perhaps you need help transporting the deceased from one place to another. I wouldn't underestimate the value of transportation. This is something best left up to the professionals. Otherwise, you have to think about details like do you throw the body in the back seat or trunk? How do you get the body from the car to wherever you are going to put them in the house? Do you use a Dolly or a wheel barrel? If there are stairs involved, how are you going to get the cadaver up and down the stairs without dinging your walls? I hate dings in my walls.

To me the difference between a good at-home funeral and a disaster lies in those details. From what I read, a good funeral parlor will give you a loaner casket for transportation or you can rent one. You don't need a good one if your beloved is becoming mulch or if you are planning cremation.

Oh, and for the record, and this is important: you cannot do your own cremation! It doesn't matter how hot you can get the grill or fireplace, this is still against the law throughout the country except in those backwoods areas where you can still marry your first cousin. Also, remember to get all the right permits for a do-it-yourself event. You have to check with the county and state to make things legal.

I cannot imagine that a do-it-yourself event is an easy task to accomplish. It's not a fun project to tackle like remodeling your own bathroom. If you screw up this event, you will never live it down – so to speak.

Driving my Husband

I had a busy day, so when my husband came home from work I suggested that we go get dinner at one of the local sports bars. He jumped at the chance since he could watch baseball at the bar. I even sweetened the pot and offered to drive.

My husband is not always that enthusiastic when I offer to be behind the wheel, but if he is going to have a few beers, he will agree to sit in my passenger seat – you know the place where even the most devout atheists find God. He exaggerates. It's not that my husband does not like my driving; he just likes his driving better.

I want to state for any police officers who may read this that I am a careful driver. My husband and I just differ on driving strategy. My strategy is simple: I put the key in the ignition, put the car in drive -- well, unless I am backing out of my driveway, and I go. My husband's strategy or strategies are far more complex. He has a different strategy for the highway, local roads, and country driving. You name the type of thoroughfare, he has a strategy.

I blame this on the fact that he is an engineer, and engineers plan out everything. When my husband is in the passenger seat while I am behind the wheel, he constantly gives me advice.

If I am on the highway, he tells me to always think two moves ahead. I just nod and pretend to listen. In reality what I want to say is "What are we playing -- freaking chess?" I just want to get from point A to point B in the least amount of time.

Another habit he has is watching my speedometer. He leans over every few minutes to see how fast I am going. "Okay, you're over 80, take it down a notch." This inevitably leads to the cruise control fight. I don't use cruise control, and he does not understand why when it keeps one's speed at an even pace and saves gas. My reason for not liking cruise control is clear to me. I like my feet to have a job when I am driving. That's why there are pedals, and I feel more in control when my feet are on those pedals.

Anyway, let me just get to our dinner out and our short drive which should have been an uneventful one. The bar is literally a mile-and-a-half from my house. However, I was driving with a temporary disability. I was having a balance and hearing issue. I had gone swimming in the morning, and I had water in my ear, and I could not get it out for anything. I did the hopping on one foot move, the pulling on my ear lobe, the swimmer's ear medicine, but nothing worked. So, all day long, I was tipping left.

While I was driving to the bar, I kept jerking my head to see if I could force the water out because it was making me crazy. Anyway, while trying to get the water out of my ear, I missed the entrance for the restaurant, and out of instinct, I slammed on my brakes and made a screeching turn into the exit.

This was not good strategy according to my husband and the guy who happened to be driving out of the exit at the time, and both of them made their feelings quite evident. I do admit that driving in the exit was not the smartest of moves, but there was no accident or confrontation, so I did not see the big deal.

We had a nice relaxing dinner, and after two beers my husband had forgotten about the whole drive to the bar. On the way home, I pulled out onto the main road and was minding my own business when the sports car behind me illegally crossed the double yellow line and passed me. Apparently, he was in a hurry. His impatience did not pay off, and he had to stop at the next red light with me behind him.

"What's your strategy here?" My husband asked.

"Well, I was thinking of waiting for the light to turn green and then maybe...*moving?*"

He had another strategy which involved me cutting around this guy and slowing up to make him late for wherever he was going. It was very complicated and with one ear out of commission, and my balance in question, I didn't think it was doable, and I told my husband so. I think he was disappointed.

I confess that I am not averse to telling someone off when driving. I will honk my horn and curse at people under my breath all the time. But I do not chase people or try to teach them a lesson. I just think that is asking for trouble.

Much to my husband's disappointment, I let the offending driver off without any punishment. He eventually got over it. But twice last night, he enlightened me on how he would have handled the evil, illegal passer. I ignored him. We are now friends again, but next time we go to that bar, he is driving.

The Hot Tub Oasis

If I look back over the years, I will say, without a doubt, that the best home improvement we ever made was my hot tub. Did you notice I used the word "my"? It's not like I don't share it. I do, but it's my baby. It's my place to go and forget about the world.

I know it sounds indulgent, but everyone deserves a way to relax. Some people mix martinis or have a shot of bourbon after a hard day – well, I do that too – but usually that's only on the weekend or if my day included me getting annoyed at anyone – at all.

I'm sorry; I am already off the track. Let me get back to the hot tub. When we first contemplated this oasis, I didn't want an outdoor spa. I wanted to redo my bathroom and put in one of those big whirlpool tubs that promised to melt away my aches and pains. I dreamed of the spa jets whirling me into a state of bliss. I envisioned a master bath suite where I could dim the lights, play soft music, light aromatherapy candles and soak away my stress. Of course, in this fantasy, my tub would be next to this amazing glass wall that offered me a view of the stars and romantic moonlit sky.

The reality of the situation was this: My old house was designed for small people. The bedrooms can barely hold a queen-size bed, the closets were designed back in the day when people owned two sets of clothes, and the bathroom-- well--the builder had only practical purposes in mind for this space. Not only is this lavatory not spa material, but there could never be a glass wall unless I want to give my old neighbor a cheap thrill.

Knowing indoor renovation was not an option, my husband and I decided to look to our outdoors instead, and we put the hot tub under the covered porch in the yard. Now, I can commune with nature and relax under the stars while getting that massage I dreamed about. The tub truly is an oasis. It has lights so I can change the color of the water with a touch of a button to fit my mood. I like all the colors except the "red". The red light makes the water look like Jaws has been swimming around and devouring unsuspecting hot tub soakers. Yes, the tub is a year-round retreat where I melt away the anxieties in my life.

Then, a few months ago, a horrible thing happened. My jets started acting up. They stopped making their smooth "vroom" sound and instead were making a jerky "vroom – klunk" sound. At first, I thought it was because I had just emptied and refilled my tub, and my baby had to get used to the new water. But it continued. My tub sounded as if it were gasping for breath.

Sheer panic set in. I called the repairman immediately, but he couldn't get out to my house for a week. A week without my tub – what would I do? I had withdrawals. I wanted to sink into my 102 degrees of paradise, but it could not be. I was devastated.

"Why don't you take a bubble bath?" my husband queried.

"You want me to soak in that ancient bathroom tub? You want me to think about a bath without jets? And, I'm sorry, but there is no room on that bathtub to set down my wine glass or a scented candle!"

He pointed out that for 15 years I never had those jets or a place to put my wine glass or scented aromatherapy candles. I tried to explain that once you have jets and the lifestyle those jets provide, there is no going back. This is just the way a hot tub works. It gently takes you in and makes itself indispensable.

My husband wasn't getting my logic at all until I equated my love for my hot tub to his love for his big TV. Boy, once I put my argument in man-vernacular, he understood. He felt my pain. I think I saw a few tears well up in his eyes. Then, he took unexpected action: he called the spa company and asked them to move up the repair date.

The repairman came and saw the problem immediately. He assured me it would be a quick fix, and he was right. When my jets started up again and I heard that melodic hum, I was swept away with emotion. The repairman left knowing he had done a good deed.

With my hot tub fixed, I can once again sit outside and gaze at the stars. I love the crisp air cooling my face while the warm water soothes my body except during sleet storms when freezing rain pelts me in the face.

My 83-year-old neighbor is curious about the hot tub too. He said his wife has some back trouble, and he was wondering how the jets would work for her. I instinctively invited her over to try out the tub.

He jumped on that invite like a tiger jumps on raw meat. Then, my older gentleman neighbor said those words I will always remember.

"We don't have bathing suits anymore. Can we go in naked?"

I have to say I was not expecting this question. I never pursued that invitation again. I don't mean to be critical, but there are some things that are best left to the imagination.

The Fortune Cookie

When my daughter was home for her last school break, she had a yen for steamed dumplings, so off we went to her favorite Chinese Restaurant. After a nice meal, the waiter brought us our complimentary fortune cookies. My husband opened his and read his fortune aloud first. According to the cookie, he was headed for a promotion, a new romance and a long life filled with happiness. I was a little perturbed. He gets a promotion, and some new chickie gets to cash in on the loot from that promotion. I guarantee if that happens, he will not be enjoying a long, happy life.

I put aside my consternation for a moment to hear my daughter's fortune. The cookie said that she will be finding joy wherever she goes, and her personality will give her the courage to take risks that will pay off in her life. I liked this fortune. All mothers want to hear about their kids' bright futures.

And then I cracked open my cookie and this is what it said: "You will be invited to sing at a karaoke bar."

That was my fortune. I swear. My family gets predictions of happiness, wealth, romance mingled with a bit of adultery, and I get a trip to a stinking karaoke bar? Of all the fortune cookies I have opened in my life--and there have been many--this was the lamest. Technically, it's not even a fortune. It's a comment on my social life, and it is an inaccurate comment because if the fortune cookie writer knew me, he or she would know I cannot carry a tune, and no one in their right mind would ever invite me to a karaoke bar to sing unless that bar was filled with people that the party host wanted to torture or drive insane!

Not satisfied with my cookie prognostication, I asked my waiter for a new cookie. Luckily, he knows us so he was more than happy to give me another. This time as I read my fortune, I had a focused audience. My daughter, husband, our waiter, the people at the table next to ours, who could not stop laughing at the karaoke prediction, and the restaurant owner all gathered to see what wisdom my cookie would impart.

And this was the fortune inside my new cookie, and again, I am not lying: "You will have a mole removed in the next few months."

Who the hell is writing fortune cookies these days? Has the pool of writers for fortune cookies become so depleted that the cookie companies have had to recruit copywriters from the American Medical Association? Perhaps my next fortune cookie will tell me the results of my pap smear. If the cookie companies are that hard up for writers, I know several freelancers who wouldn't mind the gig.

Call me a fortune cookie purist, but I like the old-fashioned fortunes that made me feel as if Confucius himself wrote them. These new fortune cookies have none of the traditional appeal. Fortune cookies are supposed to be about hope and whimsy. I know times change. I can go along with change. I didn't get upset when the fortunes in the cookies started to have lucky lottery numbers printed on them. And I didn't complain when the cookies started to have a Chinese "word of the day" on the fortune either.

Hey, it is a global economy, and since communist China is now secretly embracing capitalism, I guess knowing Chinese is a good thing. Plus, learning the language from a cookie is a lot cheaper than buying the Rosetta Stone language series.

I admit that my family and I got a kick out of my fortunes. I laughed so hard that I literally cried, and when this happens to me, my daughter always follows suit. While we were laughing our metaphorical cookies off, I noticed the owner of the restaurant was not quite as amused. I guess she is a fortune cookie purist too. She explained that she bought the cookies from a new vendor, but they had assured her that the fortunes would display dignified messages. I tried to make her feel better, and told her that the messages, while not dignified, might prove helpful. If you think about it, the fortune put in my head a health tip that might benefit me down the road.

She appreciated me being a good sport and told me that if I was interested, she had a karaoke machine that she could bring to the restaurant, and I could sing there if I wanted. I thanked her for the opportunity but graciously declined. I didn't want to be responsible for driving her business into the ground.

Well, it has been a few months since I received the karaoke and mole fortunes. I posted them on my refrigerator for those days when I need a quick laugh. This week, we went back to the Chinese restaurant, and at the end of the meal, we got our cookies again. My husband's read "To lose a dream is to lose your soul." That was a nice one and there were no gold-digging tramps in the picture, so I liked it. My daughter's said that she would embark on a new life adventure in a new place which was interesting because she might have to move for a job, and mine...well, mine said "I am uncomplicated and easily manipulated."

Note to myself: Switch to Indian food.

A Parent's Guide to Body Art

Last week, my daughter and I were chit chatting in the hot tub when she brought up the topic of tattoos. At first, I thought I didn't hear her correctly since the water was bubbling in my ears, so I sat up straight and said,

"What? Did you say tattoos – on you?"

"Not me! Good God, Mother, I know your feelings on me getting inked!"

My daughter knows I do not approve of her getting a tattoo. In fact, it is more than disapproval; I have a signed contract that says she can't have a tattoo.

Yes, you read right. This legal contract was the best parental victory of my life. This is how it came to be. Picture it: a 15-year-old girl eyeing sparkly belly button rings in the jewelry store at the Jersey shore. She turned to me and said,

"Mom, I really want my belly button pierced. Can't you talk to Dad and get him to say okay?"

"Well, if you would show a little more enthusiasm with school this coming year, I could probably get Daddy to go along with it, but I am talking First Honors – and no detentions. And maybe then for your 16th birthday, we can see."

"I can do that," she assured me.

"No detentions! Did you hear that part?" I reiterated.

I had to reiterate that part because, frankly, my daughter was the queen of detentions. I can't remember a year, including Pre-K, where she did not have to sit for at least one detention. In her defense, her detentions were mostly due to her propensity to disagree vocally with school protocol. She wasn't disrespectful - just opinionated. For the record, I have no idea where she gets this trait. It must be from her father's side.

Anyway, when her 16th birthday came around, she reminded me of my promise of the belly button piercing. I said I would check with her father, who I thought would be a stand up guy and say no way, but he didn't. I stood there with my mouth open in shock as he gave his approval.

"You are going to let them put a hole in my baby's belly? Look at that belly!" I yelled as I threw her baby book in his face.

"It's a belly button. Would you rather her get her tongue or nipple pierced?"

The thought of either of those things made me want to throw up, so I relented – not happily, but I did. What I was not prepared for was that I had to go with her and watch some stranger put a hole through her perfect little belly button. It had to be me because my husband passes out whenever any kind of needle comes near a human body. His fear of needles was part of the reason why I went drug free during childbirth. Yes, no drugs made the whole labor process difficult, but I have to admit that the mileage I have gotten from that guilt trip turned out to be better than I could have ever imagined, so the pain was well worth it.

Anyway, I made inquiries as to the best place to get this belly-button procedure done. Another mom recommended a studio called "World of Body Art". She could attest that the artists at this facility were both talented and hygienic. So, I made an appointment and there we met "Joe" who explained how he would pierce my baby's belly – that cute little belly that I kissed and rubbed with baby lotion in an effort to keep it so soft and rash free.

At first I didn't like Joe. He looked like a bigger version of Willie Nelson with lots of piercings and tattoos. His office had pictures of all the body parts that one can pierce. As I stared at this walking work of inked art, I have to admit that I was comforted to see so much jewelry pinned to his body because it showed me he believed in his profession even though he did sort of look like he spent too many years hanging out with the Hell's Angels. I am not trying to insult that fine upstanding motorcycle club in any way here, but I think that they might even admit that some of their members have a tendency to go overboard on the body painting at times.

Anyway, once Joe started to talk, I felt more comfortable. He was actually a very well spoken individual, and he had a degree from Dartmouth. It's funny how an Ivy League education makes all the difference in situations like this. I was feeling really good until he told me how the 60s and 70s did a number on him. I wanted to ask him to explain further, but I didn't want to upset him while he was holding a needle to my daughter's tummy.

Anyway, the piercing took a long time because Miss Ballerina had really tight abs which made it difficult to push the needle through. When she grimaced; I grimaced. When she started to tear; I started to tear. When she maintained a sense of calm, I did not. Finally, it was over. Joe gave us antiseptic, and we went home. Although my daughter was glad she did it, she admitted that if by any chance this piercing got infected, she would never do it again.

For three days, that stupid piercing throbbed. I thought for sure I was going to have to take her to the emergency room and admit what a lousy parent I was. I dreamed that social services was going to come and take her away because I let her get an infected belly button. In the middle of the night I would go into her room and say, "Let me see your belly button." Finally, she could take my worrying no more, and screamed,

"What would you do if I got a tattoo?"

Well, that's when I got the legal idea. I had my friend who is an attorney make up a document that said my daughter could not get another body piercing or tattoo. I shoved it in front of my daughter's face and said "Sign it." I expected an argument but none came. I think she liked the idea that she had an out if there was any peer pressure to get any other body part "skewered". I had the contract notarized, and then I framed it. Yep, and this contract was no slipshod agreement. It did not end when she turned 18 or 21. No, this contract specifically states that under no circumstances will she get any other piercings or tattoos until I am dead. Yep, D-E-A-D! After I croak she is free and clear, but until that time, her body remains ineligible for inkings and piercings.

Fast forward six years and my daughter and I are in the hot tub and I heard the word "tattoo". She told me how some of her friends got the Penn State paw print tattooed on their hip, and she looked at me.

"Am I dead? Do I look dead to you?"

She just looked at me and rolled her eyes.

Well, I guess that contract did last a good, long time. I could be open for some re-negotiation. Maybe, I will get a tattoo first and make her go with me to see how they do it. I bet I could cry really loud if I had to. Perhaps fear might prove to be a better deterrent than any contract ever written.

The Literary Elite at Starbucks

I decided I needed a quick pick-me-up, so I headed to Starbucks. I was sitting with my coffee and crossword puzzle at a table in the corner when I started to eavesdrop on the conversation between the two people at the tables next to mine. Technically, it was not eavesdropping as they were both talking pretty loudly, and their conversation was hard to avoid. Each of these people had a laptop in front of them, and each was supposedly busy creating the next great novel or movie or whatever.

I have to admit that right away I got intimidated. I know that sounds silly, but people who write in public on laptops just do that to me. They seem so artsy and sure of themselves. It's not that I can't write in public. I was a reporter, so I had to learn to write in the most unusual places such as the state penitentiary for men. I always say if you can write a story and make a deadline during a prison lockdown, you can write anywhere.

I should explain that I didn't go to the prison because I liked the creative atmosphere. The prison was part of my beat, so I had an obligation to go there at least once a week. Every once in a while there was a security problem that resulted in a lockdown and me spending more time in the prison than anticipated. For all of the inmates who might have been paroled since my last visit, I just want to say that I am NOT making fun of you or your confinement here, and I wish to thank you for all the kind compliments about my appearance you gave me through the years of your unfortunate incarceration.

Anyway, back to the Starbucks writers. They started to discuss dialogue and plot development and blah, blah, blah, and I started to think how boring my writing was. They were talking about creating literature while my last assignment was writing about the vampire craze and how it affects the retail world. It's easy to see why I would think my work lacks excitement although I did get an invitation from a California store owner who asked me to come to her store to witness firsthand a blood-drinking ceremony.

As I sat at my table pretending to do my puzzle, I started to wonder how these writers got work done surrounded by so much pastry. If I did my writing in a Starbucks, I would be 400 pounds. No, I would be 400 pounds and unpublished because all I would do is eat the baked goods!

As I continued to listen to their conversation, the "What Kind Of Writer Are You?" drama started to play in my head. Most writers have some kind of individual drama that plays inside their brains on occasion. Mine usually does a matinee and evening performance on a daily basis. This is how it can go:

Insane self: "You are a waste of a writer. Look how boring your assignments are!

Sane self: "Shut up! I have tons of publishing credits to my name."

Insane self: "Yes, but your books will never be featured on Oprah's Book Club!"

Sane self: "I don't need Oprah! Wait... did I just say that? I'm sorry, Oprah. I do need you! Don't be mad at me! Oh God, I think I need to switch to decaf!"

Yep. It is sad but that is but one act of my internal play. I have another observation about the Starbucks writers. I spent an hour there and those two writers did not write one word. Yes, they talked writer talk, but they did not do writer work. I guess I should not jump to conclusions or scoff, because every writer is different in their work routines. Really, how do I know that one of these literary minds before me might not become the next Hemingway or Danielle Steele?

Okay, I admit I read Danielle Steele. She is my beach buddy. There is something about the ocean that makes me want to read sex and violence books big time. I'm sure Freud had a theory on it, but it's my vacation and I can do whatever I want, so don't judge me. There are plenty of closet Danielle Steele fans out there.

After an hour in Starbucks, I left those two writers to their supposed craft. I went home to my messy, messy desk, dug through notes, put on Frank Sinatra and began to type. I guess my routine is not that much different than the coffee shop writers' routine after all. They have music playing in the background; I have music playing in the background. They have coffee; I have coffee. They have baked goods; I have a stash of chocolate doughnuts hidden in the freezer waiting to be devoured. What can I say? Some days, chocolate doughnuts are the only inspiration I need.

Every Dog Deserves a Ball...or Two

I will admit that my dogs are spoiled. I have a family room filled with their toys. We have birthday parties for them; they eat sirloin steak from time to time; and their lives in general are more relaxed and pampered than mine. However, even my spoiling has limits. There have been a few pet products that have come on the market in recent years that I refuse to buy.

I will not buy my dog clothes. Okay, they wear matching bandanas, and for our Christmas card photo, they may sport an appropriate hat, but that is where I draw the line. They do not wear dresses or angora sweaters, and there is no way in hell that I am coughing up money for dog Snuggies so my pooches can be cuddly and warm while watching TV. Isn't their fur their own built-in Snuggie?

I also refuse to polish their nails or make them wear diamond-studded collars, and last but so NOT least, they do not ride in a stroller. Yes, I make my dogs walk. I know that sounds cold and callous, but my dogs walk next to me on a leash or they run free in the yard. It was only recently that I discovered there were such things as dog strollers. I remember the day I first encountered one. I was in an antique store when a young couple came in pushing a pretty pink stroller. Being a baby lover, I said

"Congratulations. How old is your baby?"

"Six months," they responded simultaneously. I could hear the pride in their voices. Then the mom lifted the mesh that protected the little one from the sun (her words not mine) to show me her little miracle, and I literally gasped out loud. In the stroller was a freaking dog! At first, I thought this couple just had a really ugly, hairy kid, but then I realized the ugly hairy kid was a Pomeranian.

"You wheel around your dog?" I asked.

"Yes, walking is so hard on her little legs," the woman said.

"She's a dog. That's why she has four legs."

"But she is such a precious baby!" she countered.

I didn't say anything further because spittle had started to form around her mouth (the woman's not the dog's) and her eyes began to twitch, and well, she started to scare me, so I backed away from those people and left the store hoping that before they decide to produce a human child, they get their mental states checked by some kind of expert.

Soon after the stroller encounter, I discovered that those pet owners were not an oddity. No, many pet owners have jumped on the dog stroller bandwagon. Sometimes, when I have my dogs at the park and a dog stroller family comes bopping along, my own pooches look at me with eyes that say,

"Hey, what the hell is wrong with you? We want wheels too! How come we have to walk?"

I try to explain to my pooches the importance of a good daily cardio workout, but it's difficult for them to believe me when they see the pretty sparkly canine carriages with the anti-mosquito netting pass by us on the walking paths.

After I accepted the pet stroller's popularity, I had to wonder what the next new pet product would be. Well, I wonder no longer. While talking with another pet owner the other day, I learned about Neuticles. What are Neuticles? Well, hold on because your mouth is going to drop open.

Neuticles are testicular implants for dogs that have been neutered.

Yep, if you are the owner of a male dog and you are worried about the emotional impact that neutering will have on him, you can purchase Neuticles. Ranging in price from $94 for a generic set to $1,799 for a custom-fitted pair, Neuticles are designed to have the look and feel of the real – um, what shall I say here? Package. Yes, package is a good word.

Now, you can get your male dog's testicles whacked and not feel the guilt of taking away his manhood. Oops, sorry for that imagery. I know how sensitive men are when it comes to any kind of injury afflicting their best friends below the belt. Yes, veterinarians can now make it so Fido can get "fixed" but still have a visible pair to show the world. While not all vets have embraced the use of Neuticles regarding the implant procedure as unnecessary surgery, other vets have taken the ball--so to speak--and run with it, because it might make owners less squeamish about getting their male dog neutered.

I can hear what women are saying. "This is a typical male response to neutering. Go anyway near a man's boys or his dog's boys and they fall apart like babies."

Yes, it's true that men have a particularly difficult time getting their male dogs neutered. They truly empathize with their dog's pain, and they project their own fear about losing their manhood onto their dogs, but guess what, Ladies? The predominant buyers of Neuticles are women. Who knew women could be so sensitive about that area. I guess that dispels the old adage that size doesn't matter-- well, on a dog anyway.

Snuggie vs. Forever Lazy in the Battle to Stay Warm

As I was flipping through the TV channels at 3 AM, I saw it! Yes, I didn't believe it was possible but there it was staring me in the face. At first, I thought it was the brandy that I drank a few hours before coming back to haunt me, but no, it was real. Finally, there is a new product that will bring the Snuggie® to its knees.

Yes, in an effort to outdo and update the Snuggie, the blanket with sleeves that millions of suckers bought and thought was just grand, some inventor has come up with a Snuggie that you step into. And while this TV commercial goes on about the revolutionary design of this new product, I had to think to myself (again, it could have been the brandy): "Isn't this just adult feetie pajamas minus the feeties?"

If you have not seen it yet, the zip up loungewear or the Forever Lazy® will be coming to your late-night and Sunday TV airwaves soon. This "new" cuddly outfit boasts a thick fuzzy, coat -- or the technical term -- polar fleece. You step into it and zip it up and you will be warm and toasty throughout all activities, and you don't even have to unzip and step out of it when nature beckons. No, the Forever Lazy comes with "Zippered Hatches in Front and Back, for Great Escapes When Duty Calls".

That is the best copywriting I have ever seen. Have we become that lazy a society that we can't pull down our pants to use the potty anymore? The other advantage that this product has over the Snuggie is its claim that you can wear it anywhere. Yes, you can wear it to picnics, camping and my absolute favorite – tailgating because nothing goes better in the stadium parking lot port-o-potties than a fleece suit with a flap in the back for when you need to squat.

I know I am being harsh and close minded about this product especially when the commercials show this party of about 10 adults, all donned in their Forever Lazy attire, having fun singing and dancing at a tailgate. When I see this commercial, I think: First, I am willing to bet these people were never the cool kids in high school. Second, I live in Philly. I can't imagine the abuse I would take if I went tailgating to an Eagles' game in adult pajamas with a back flap. It wouldn't matter which of the three attractive Forever Lazy colors I chose, I would still get beaten up.

It's ridiculous. I am sorry. This is not an adult product. After age 12, you don't wear pajamas outside the house unless you are looking to score one of those 48-hour observation periods at the local psychiatric hospital. And I am being generous in my age limit. By age 12, if you are going somewhere where it's going to be cold, you put on warm clothes. You don't hang out in your pajamas with a flap. And I am going to stick up for the Snuggie here, and I swore I would never do that, but at least the Snuggie goes over your clothes. It doesn't become your clothes. I think the Forever Lazy is your clothes. Well, guys could wear their jeans underneath because the front flap would lead to the zipper which leads to their – well, you know – but it's a bit more complicated for a woman. If a woman is wearing clothes underneath the Forever Lazy, the back flap does nothing. The pants still have to come down, so should I assume that the creators of this product want us to wear this pajama outfit as a bona fide-wear-it-in-public ensemble?

I know it comes in pink, black and blue or some choice like that. And they say that one of these colors will satisfy everyone. Well, I don't care what color I choose, I can't imagine it being an attractive look. It's baggy and it has a flap. Just wearing an outfit with a flap sends out the wrong message. It doesn't say "I like to be cozy." No, it says, "I have a flap, and I am prepared to use it." Is that really what you want people to think about you? Is this a good date outfit? Hm. Maybe on the date thing, it is. It is easy access. I will have to research that.

I know that the Forever Lazy will be a hit because the Snuggie was. I was amazed at the Snuggie's rise in popularity because to be honest, it's nothing more than a backwards robe. But, the Forever Lazy will also gain momentum and then, like the Snuggie and its successful copycats, it will be offered in professional and college team colors.

Get ready for the Forever Lazy explosion. One day, as you watch your favorite football team on TV, you will look at the crowd and no longer see fans wearing their favorite players' jerseys. No, you will see a sea of people in Forever Lazy attire enjoying their beer and their easy escape flaps. I don't know, but something is really wrong with that picture.

Flustered Over Flushing

I believe a special Nobel Prize should go to the guy who invented the automatic flush toilet. I am serious about this as I have a great deal of experience with public bathrooms. We travel up and down the east coast to visit family all year long. Through the years of this highway travel, I have gagged at many of the women's bathrooms at the rest stops that dot the American landscape. No matter what state the scene is always the same.

The first thing a woman notices when entering a public bathroom is the yellow cone bearing both the English and Spanish translation of the words "Caution, wet floor" that always sits in the middle of the stall aisle. Do people who use public bathrooms only speak English and Spanish? What about those women who do not speak either language? Do they get to slip and fall on the germ-filled floor because they don't understand the words on the cone?

Those who can read the cone, tiptoe around it as they make their way to the bathroom stalls. Then, they gingerly push in each door hoping to find a stall with a clean toilet. It is like a scene from a horror movie where the stupid college chick starts to go into the room where she just heard all the strange noises. Even though she does not know what waits for her on the other side. In a public bathroom, we pretty much know what's waiting for us on the other side of that door. Allow me to say that I don't understand how in a country which is filled with so many potty-trained adults, there can be so many women who can't aim into the toilet. I know it's hard to squat, but really, it's not that difficult a task.

Let me get back to the point of this whole thing. About 10 years ago, I started to notice the arrival of automatic-flush toilets in the public rest stops.

"This is interesting" I thought when I first noticed the no-hands flush system. I was a little unsure of the little red light attached to the toilet. I figured it was a sensor that told the toilet when I was done, but the paranoid person inside of me had to wonder if a camera was attached. Once I realized, that no one was filming my activities, (well, maybe with the exception of a few rest stops on the New Jersey Turnpike), I relaxed. I really liked that I did not have to touch anything near that toilet.

Then, the automatic bathroom people came up with the automatic sinks. These were good too, but I never met an automatic sink that acted consistently. Sometimes, I can wave my hands under the sink once and water just flows out. Other times, I can wave my hands, my arms or even a magic wand and no water comes out, and there is no manual backup system. If the automatic sink does not flow, you get no water. The same is true for the automatic soap dispensers and the newest addition to the public bathroom, the automatic towel holder. There are times when I have so much arm action going on in one bathroom visit that I actually get a full aerobic workout and I need a whiff of my asthma inhaler before I can go on with the rest of my day.

I truly appreciate the no-touch technology in the public bathrooms, but I do have one suggestion for rest stops, stores, restaurants or anyone else with the automatic devices. If you have an automatic toilet, have an automatic towel dispenser and an automatic soap dispenser. If you mix and match automatic and manual, you confuse people.

I was having breakfast with my friend, Ginny. Ginny is a smart woman. She has an MBA and runs her own PR firm. I need to emphasize her intelligence before I tell this story. After drinking several cups of coffee, Ginny had to use the ladies room. Five minutes went by, and she didn't come back. At the 10-minute mark, I grew concerned. I went back to the bathrooms just to make sure she didn't fall in. Just as I was ready to push the door open, she emerged – frustrated but alive. It seems she had been stymied by the bathroom fixtures. The sink and paper towel holder were automatic but the toilet and soap dispenser were not. Her bathroom visit was not pleasant.

My final word on automatic bathroom fixtures: We women take a long time as it is in the bathroom. Make our public bathroom treks a little more user-friendly and tell us what is automatic and what is not. Post a sign and tell us if we should flush or not flush, if we should turn on the faucet or if we should do a dance to the bathroom gods to get the freaking towel out of the dispenser. Anyway, a little direction can go a long way to a positive potty experience.

My Refrigerator and the Parallel Universe

My coffee creamer had somehow re-located itself to the back of my refrigerator. As I removed the soy milk, the orange juice, the tomato juice, and the ten other items that stood in front of my beloved creamer, I realized it was time to clean out this old monstrosity once again. I do not understand how this appliance gets so crowded with stuff. We are only three people in this house, and I do try to empty it out regularly... well, occasionally...okay, twice a year...maybe, less. I don't know. I don't keep track.

So, I am not sure what came over me, but after I found my creamer, I decided it was time to do the refrigerator purge right then and there. I started with the top shelf and worked my way down. Refrigerators are amazing. They are the black hole of appliances. There is a whole Twilight Zone thing going on inside that beast. I can put a container or jar on a shelf and then it disappears. My theory on this is that it gets sucked into some kind of parallel refrigerator universe. That jar or container is not seen again for months until it is spit out of the alternate universe and left for dead in the very back corner of the middle shelf where no eyes ever dare to look.

I have to say that the alternate refrigerator universe was busy this time around. As I reached my hands into my old appliance, I came across several of those disposable leftover containers. I lifted the cover on one which sent my gag reflex into overdrive, and I had to head over to the sink until dry heaves passed. After I composed my stomach, I took the other three disposable containers and chucked them in the trash. Then, I found an open can of Betty Crocker chocolate frosting.

"Ooh, I remember this," I said aloud. "This isn't that old. A few months tops." I opted to keep the frosting because to me it is sacred food, and I remembered when I purchased this can. I wasn't baking – God, no! No, I got this one during an emotional PMS episode when I was simultaneously experiencing a "my writing career is in the toilet" syndrome. When I get hit with a double whammy like that, I seek comfort in my two best friends: Betty Crocker and the Pillsbury Dough Boy.

I can eat an entire can of frosting without blinking an eye, so the mystery in this case is not when I bought the frosting, but how is it that some frosting remained? Frankly, I was happy to see the frosting, so I made a cozy place for it in the fridge. Instead, I threw out condiments, pickles, olives, salad dressings, wasabi sauce and a tub of fat free cream cheese that I found in one of the secret bins on the fridge door. I opened one leftover – or what I assumed to be a leftover wrapped in aluminum foil and had to dry heave again, so I decided it was best to throw out anything else wrapped in foil as well.

After I was done with the purge, I wiped down all the shelves with anti-bacterial cleaner and stuck a new box of baking soda on a shelf to keep my fridge from developing foul odors. Maybe, I shouldn't put in the baking soda. Maybe it does too good a job. Maybe, if some of the smells actually hit my nostrils, I would clean out this old beast sooner.

I love when my fridge is clean and sparkly. Every time I go into the kitchen, I open the door just to see how shiny it looks. Of course, my family opens the door and says, "We have no food. We need food." I will buy food for it, but for just a day or two, I like to see that monstrosity neat and clean. Once I buy food, the parallel refrigerator universe will once again rear its ugly head and claim my food as its own, and the cycle of refrigerator purging will have to begin again.

Wedding Dreams and Nightmares

I have become addicted to two wedding-themed shows on television. The first, *Say Yes to the Dress,* focuses on the sales consultants and clients of Kleinfeld's, a renowned bridal salon in New York City. During each episode, we are introduced to brides and their entourages who have come to the famous store in search of the perfect bridal dress which is not always easy to find.

Although during some episodes, there are tears and screaming, it is nothing compared to my second favorite wedding show, *Bridezillas*, which drives home the point that there is someone for everyone in this world even if that someone is a crazy, diva bitch who thinks the world revolves around her.

I don't know why I watch this show. I think I watch it hoping that the men, who are engaged to these shallow and very scary women, somehow locate their manhood, which obviously has been stolen from them, and tell their fiancées that they won't be making the trip down the aisle. Every week I watch, and every week I realize that love is blind and this is why divorce law is such a lucrative profession.

I watch *Say Yes to the Dress* with my daughter. I get nervous watching this show with her because she thinks $4,000 for a wedding dress is the minimum she wants to spend, which requires me to ask, "Have you met your father?" I refuse to watch *Bridezillas* with her because I am afraid she will look at one of these women and say, "Wow, she is my hero."

The women on *Bridezillas* are nothing short of psycho. I know that is not a politically correct term, but this is the only word to describe them. They yell, curse, rant, cry, threaten, cause property damage and scare people to death all because they want to be the star in their own wedding show. I think someone has forgotten to tell these women that the wedding is about marriage and not a chance to be Idi Amin in a dress. And if it's not the bride screaming and carrying on, it's the future mother-in-law carrying on about how the bride must have drugged her son to make him marry her. Okay, I tend to stick up for the mothers-in-law here. If I had a son and he came home with one of these Bridezillas, I would have to cut him loose.

Anyway, as we watched the most recent episode of *Say Yes to the Dress*, my daughter and I chatted about her dream wedding. The problem with us is that we are very different people. While I would choose to get married in a meadow somewhere and have a big picnic for a reception, she is hoping I can convince the President to let us have the Rose Garden. With compromise in mind and even though there is not a wedding in sight, I grabbed my laptop and began to search what types of weddings have become popular in recent years. Why? Because I am a reporter and that is what reporters do.

The *Romeo and Juliet Wedding*: This is not just two people dressed up like the famous duo. No, this is in Verona, Italy on the actual balcony that inspired Shakespeare to write his masterpiece. There are a few glitches for us with this one. First: We have a tough enough time getting our family to come from New York to Philly to visit us, so I have serious doubts that they would fly to Verona just to see her say her I Do's. Second: The Romeo and Juliet theme sounds romantic, but let's think about the plot here. Sure, they were in love, but it didn't last very long, and they both wound up killing themselves. Call me old-fashioned but a double suicide might cast a shadow over an otherwise enjoyable event.

Movie Theme Weddings: It's no surprise to me that sci-fi themes are quite a common theme in weddings. A couple can have anything including a Captain Kirk wannabe officiating the ceremony to guests dressing up in *Star Wars* outfits. I can't see my daughter choosing a *Star Wars* wedding which is sad because I think her father would like to walk her down the aisle wearing a Darth Vader outfit. Also nixed from her movie list are *Gone with the Wind* and *Wizard of Oz* themes. Again, the backdrop of blown up bodies or a band of homicidal flying monkeys might not provide the festive ambiance one might want with a wedding.

Also, not allowed to be considered is anything Gothic or physically dangerous such as skydiving or riding a big roller coaster while saying vows. I put the kibosh on the physically dangerous weddings. If I am going to spend money on dresses for her and me, they are not going to be ruined by projectile vomit which will undoubtedly make its presence known when I jump from that airplane or fly upside down on the coaster.

Naked Weddings I bet you didn't think these were popular, but guess what? They are, and more resorts are offering nude wedding packages. I am happy to announce that my daughter has no interest in a nude event. While I am relieved about this, I have to admire those who opt for this "package". I think a naked wedding shows true commitment. If you are willing to marry a person after you him or her standing upright in daylight, it is true love.

Down the road, when the time comes, I think my daughter will choose a more traditional wedding approach. But I have already informed her that if she shows one sign of becoming a Bridezilla, she is on her own.

The Deli Wars

Usually, when I do my "big" grocery shopping, I ask my husband to come along so we can split up the list and get out of the supermarket as quickly as possible. During our last excursion, our first stop was the deli counter. I ripped off a ticket from the number dispenser and it said 38. I looked up and the "now serving" sign read 22. This was going to be a long wait. I am not a patient person when it comes to the deli line. I am going to say something that you might not like, but I can't stand waiting in line behind all the senior citizens, and yesterday, the majority of that line consisted of senior citizens.

Don't get self-righteous on me. I have my reasons why I have no patience with the seniors in the deli line. First, they take ten minutes to sample everything before deciding what they want. Then, after the deli person prepares their order, they examine each piece of meat to see if it is sliced to the right width. God forbid, one piece of low-sodium ham is thicker than the rest because if that happens, the order gets tossed, and the deli worker has to start all over again.

I know that many of you are saying that senior citizens do not mean to keep people waiting, but I think you are wrong. It is my sincerest belief that the goal of senior citizens in deli lines is to drive the non-senior citizen population insane. I think there is a secret AARP chapter whose main mission is the slow mental annihilation of the non-senior citizen masses, and their main weapon of choice is the supermarket deli line.

Anyway, when I saw the line at the deli counter and who was in it, I decided to use the ordering kiosk. The little computer with the touch screen takes my order, prints out a receipt and in about 20 minutes, I go back to the deli and find my order in the "pre-ordered" bin. It's a great idea which has saved me a great deal of time and possibly the lives of many older Americans.

Yesterday, my husband selected turkey breast and American cheese. American cheese is an amazing product. Where I grew up, yellow American seemed to be the more popular color choice for cheese. I never asked why it was yellow. I thought that yellow was the natural color of cheese. When I moved to Philly years ago, white American was the most popular choice of the citizenry. So, wanting to fit in, I started to buy white cheese.

I couldn't find my order in the bin. There was a bin with turkey and cheese but it was yellow cheese, so I asked the lady behind the deli counter if my order was still waiting to be done. She asked for my receipt that the kiosk printed out, and I gave it to her. Keep in mind that I was very polite, and up until this point, I did not sense any hostility from her.

She took the receipt and pointed me to the bin that had the yellow cheese. I should have just kept my mouth and ate the damn yellow cheese, but no, I had to say,

"Oh, yellow cheese, I thought I ordered the white. Can I get white instead?"

A look so evil came over her face. She leaned her head over the counter and said,

"If you didn't want the yellow cheese, you shouldn't have ordered the yellow. Can't you read?"

"I ordered white cheese," I said pointing to the receipt.

"But I sliced yellow."

I thought this was kind of rude. A few years ago, my first reaction might have been to leap over the counter and fight it out, but as I enter middle age, I am trying to become classier so I said,

"I am sorry. I probably screwed up but it's only freaking cheese."

"Do you think we have nothing but time here to redo orders?"

"I don't know; I was guessing it was your job."

I would have continued the discussion but my husband was waiting for me by the checkout, and I didn't want him to hear over the P.A. system: "Would a Mr. Cavanagh meet the police at the deli counter. Your wife is being arrested for a physical altercation with a deli person."

At the checkout line, I told him the tale of how the deli lady yelled at me. He just shook his head, but he was pretty impressed that I didn't clock her. Honestly, by the time we got to the parking lot, I was over the whole thing, but my husband was still a little ticked.

"You know, I hate how customer service is. I hate that store employees can be rude and no one cares."

I did agree with him. Would my encounter with the rude deli woman stop me from going to that supermarket? No. I am not a grudge holder. She was already angry before she ran into me, so something had to happen to make her snap at me. Who knows? Maybe she had just waited on a bus load of senior citizens who wanted their low-sodium ham cut just right.

They Don't Make Car Breakdowns Like They Used To

I had to pick up one of my friends at the car dealership where her car was getting its computer overhauled. Apparently, something went kerflooey and her turn signals would not go on if she had the radio turned on. Not being an automotive expert, I saw no reason to doubt her word especially since I have heard many similar horror stories about car computers in recent years.

I am probably cursing myself, but I have never experienced any computer malfunction with my cars. At least, I do not think so. I am not exactly sure when computers were first installed into cars, so I could be wrong. However, there was a time, when broken down cars were the story of my life. I do not think there is a highway on the east coast of the United States that has not been host to one of my breakdowns – auto, not mental. Even as a kid, our cars broke down. The big joke heading down to the Jersey shore for vacation was which one of our cars would die on the Garden State Parkway. The weird thing is it always seemed to be the one as I was riding in.

I have to say that when we did break down years ago, there always seemed to be a Good Samaritan ready and willing to help out. When my sister's Firebird decided to die in the Cheesequake Rest Area in New Jersey, a police detective from New York City pulled alongside and worked on the car for two hours. He de-crudded (I think that's the technical term) wires and tinkered with engine parts until the car started again. He would not allow us to buy him lunch or even a cup of coffee. We tried to send him a thank you gift, but when I called the precinct the next week where he said he worked, the desk sergeant said no detective by that name worked there. To this day, I cannot be sure if we had one of those guardian angel experiences that are always featured on *Unsolved Mysteries* or if we narrowly escaped a serial killer.

A while back, my husband and I were driving home from a wedding in upstate New York when our Pontiac Phoenix, (yes, the reason why lemon laws were enacted) started spewing steam. We pulled over and within minutes a man, who resembled Grizzly Adams, parked his pickup truck behind us. As someone who was born in the Bronx, my first gut reaction was to reach for the tire jack in the trunk, but as it turns out, this guy was another Good Samaritan-in-the-making. He examined our engine and saw that our fan belt had fallen off its sprockets. Then he looked me up and down and said,

"Give me your panty hose."

"Wh – what?" I stammered.

"Your panty hose. Take them off; I need them."

Once again, I thought about the tire jack. My husband instinctively stood in front of me. Then, the car savior saw my face of panic and explained what he needed my stockings for. He was going to use them to pull the fan belt and position it back on its track.

"Oh, good idea!" my husband exclaimed. "Take off your stockings and give them to him."

"We are on a highway! I am NOT taking them off."

"Go in the back seat and take them off, so we can get back on the road."

I really had a problem giving this man panty hose that I was just wearing. Come on, it is not like I was on a first name basis with him, and he didn't even buy me dinner first. Instead, in the spirit of preserving what was left of my dignity, I walked back to the trunk, unzipped my suitcase and retrieved a new pair of stockings, my black, lace-top, thigh-high stockings from Victoria's Secret. Yes, I was embarrassed to hand over these little lovelies, but I felt it was better to let the man have fantasies about me later than to have the real deal watching me strip in the backseat of my car.

Anyway, do you know that the stocking stunt worked? Grizzly Adams got the fan belt back on its sprockets, and the car was fine to make it home. I let him have my thigh highs as a gift. He laughed but both my husband and I noticed that he stuffed them in his pants pocket. Ah well, it was a small sacrifice to make for a car that runs.

Well, Grizzly Adams was another hero who wouldn't take money, but I had a feeling he was content with my stockings. I think he would have been more content if my husband offered him me, as he had that mountain-man-in-need-of-a-wife look, but luckily, those were negotiations that did not require our participation.

Fur Flies at the Sonic Drive-In

This morning, there seemed to be one crisis after another. I ran out of creamer for my coffee, one of my editors needed to vent at me about another writer, and I had a no show on a phone interview which really ticked me off because I got up at the crack of dawn to call London to talk to the guy. By noon, no amount of caffeine was going to make me productive, so I gathered my daughter and two dogs and headed to Sonic.

We love Sonic. The girls (my dogs) enjoy Sonic more than any other fast food restaurant. I think because they can interact with the help. When we go to a drive-thru, they get frustrated because they hear the server's voice over the intercom, but they don't see anyone. For my neurotic, Bambi-looking pooch, LuLu, this is especially worrisome. Voices with no bodies attached make her skittish, and she starts to shake.

But at Sonic, not only do the girls see a head, but they see an entire body as the serving staff sometimes roller skates up to our window to bring food.

Okay, there has been an instance or two when Frankie, my moose dog, has tried to relieve the server of the food before he or she has had a chance to hand it off to me. In fact, the last time we were at Sonic, the server had to bring us our order twice since Frankie's paw knocked the tray with the food out of the server's hands. While the server laughed at the incident, I was not as amused since I had to pay for the fast food meal twice and so this excursion wound up costing me as much as a sit down dinner somewhere else.

Anyway, today I took precautions and kept the girls in their seatbelts until the server skated off. Then, I carefully laid out each girl's burger so that they would have their food in front of them while my daughter and I enjoyed our lunch. It's funny how we got maybe one bite into our chicken sandwiches and both dogs were already done with their meals. Obviously, I have failed in teaching them proper table etiquette.

We tried to ignore the panting and whimpering from the back seat that easily translated into "GIVE US MORE FOOD", but it soon got to be impossible. So, I ripped off part of my sandwich, divided it into two pieces, and gave one to each dog. This is when the trouble started. One piece must have fallen on the floor of my Escape, and for some reason both dogs wanted that one piece. They dove to the floor and a Cujo moment ensued.

A Cujo moment in my house is when both dogs start to fight -- usually it's over a toy or a bone. It's never a big deal; it's just loud. I get in the middle of the two of them and yell "STOP NOW!" That command sends them off to opposite corners. Then, they feel badly about their outburst and come together and start kissing each other. However, in the small confines of the car, the STOP command had little effect. The dogs were growling, the fur was flying, the food was everywhere and my daughter and I were not helping matters by yelling as well. Finally, I jumped into the backseat and into the middle of the fray and put an end to the barking, sniping and bad behavior. When all was said and done, my nice clean escape with its newly detailed leather seats, was filled with dog hair, mashed burger pieces and splatters of ketchup. It looked like a scene from CSI: Miami.

While we thought it was a wild scene in the car, I can only imagine what the people in the car next to us thought. After the doggie altercation was over, I happened to look up to see if anyone caught the canine chaos. The two teenage guys next to us were convulsed in laughter. I cannot be sure if they were laughing at us, but unless they had some other type of comedic entertainment going on in that car, it's a pretty good bet that we were the source of their giggling.

I quickly buckled the girls back in their seatbelts and took off. I guess the road trip and the fighting was too much for them because they slept the entire drive home. When I pulled into the driveway, I let them into the backyard and they both caught sight of the same squirrel. They took off after the rodent and then stopped to play with each other in the yard. I knew then that all was forgiven. The one nice thing about dogs: they don't hold grudges. We should all take a lesson from them.

Why Must There Always Be a Big Tease?

While I was in the midst of giving birth years ago, the young medical resident, who was lucky enough to get the Christmas Day shift in labor and delivery, tried to explain to me how the hormone Oxytocin worked and how it was going to help me deliver my baby. I will admit that my mind was on other things, so his lecture failed to impress me. Now, had the nurses been able to locate an anesthesiologist who was not downing eggnog and who was willing to come to the hospital to give me drugs before that ever important "window of opportunity" closed, I might have been more receptive to learning about the wonder hormone.

That was the last time I had heard about Oxytocin – until a few days ago. I signed up to listen to this women's empowerment telephone seminar, and the speakers talked about the benefits of Oxytocin. Apparently, if a woman can find a way to increase the amount of Oxytocin in her body, she has a better chance of success. It's not a magic bullet, but it does allow women to capitalize on their strengths of warmth, compassion and making others feel at ease.

I looked up Oxytocin and discovered that it is an amazing hormone. It not only helps in childbirth, but it helps women produce milk for nursing plus it reduces stress, anxiety and blood pressure. When higher levels of the hormone are released in the body, it can increase pain thresholds and bring about a warm and fuzzy feeling toward people and animals and pretty much anything that crosses one's path.

That is why it has earned the nickname "the cuddle" hormone.

Some scientists think that Oxytocin, may be responsible for both men and women achieving stronger orgasms. Okay, not all scientists are on board with this theory, but as someone who is pro-orgasm, I will go with the scientists who believe this to be true. I'm not sure if I know anyone who is anti-orgasm, but I'm guessing those are the people who are ordered by the court to go to anger management classes.

Anyway, the women who gave the seminar kept saying there were exercises involving the Vagus nerve that can increase Oxytocin levels. So, I waited and waited for the exercises. Guess what? This info wasn't part of the free seminar. The women kept teasing about the exercises, and then they would stop and say there wasn't enough time during the hour to explain the exercises, but they said that at the end of the call there would be a surprise offer that would allow listeners to gain access to all of the secret information. They suggested that listeners stick around for the big finish – and they did not mean orgasms. No, they meant taking out a credit card and ordering stuff.

I stayed around. Later in the call, they said there were affirmations women could use that might help release Oxytocin and make women more receptive to empowerment. I waited for a sample affirmation. Again, after they told me how great these affirmations were, they said they had no time to give any free ones out on this call. For ten minutes, they told me why they had no time to tell me affirmations, but again if I listened to the entire call believing the hype there would be that surprise offer at the end that would reveal all to me.

I know these women were out to market their service, but come on, for all the time they wasted telling me what they could not tell me, they could have told me something that would help me build up my Oxytocin so that I could have really great orgasms – I mean empowerment – yeah, that's what I want-- empowerment.

You know, this is not the first teleseminar that has sucked me into giving my time for nothing. I think these seminar people would get more customers if they were more up front. I would have signed up for the whole thing if they said at the beginning:

"Okay this is the deal. You can listen for an hour and get nothing but teasers or you can sign up now, and pay us $30 and get all the information you want right away."

But they didn't. They reeled me in with quotes from women who said the telephone seminar changed their lives. I am happy for them, but, personally, I need a little more substance to have a life transformation moment.

So, am I giving up on Oxytocin? No. I already found an exercise online that would aid in releasing more Oxytocin. Would you like to know what that exercise is? I am sorry, I have no time to tell you here, but if you send me $30, the information is yours. You know, it's sort of fun holding that kind of power. I think my Oxytocin is kicking in.

The Umpire's Wife Has Been Ejected

My husband has been a baseball and fast pitch softball umpire for about 10 years. Some umpire wives go to games to see their husband's ump. Me, I rarely attend. It's not that I am not interested in his hobbies. I am. I just don't want to be ejected again. Yes, in one of his rare ejections, my husband tossed me from the field of play. I will admit that he had no choice. I have a problem when people pick on him, my daughter or my dogs.

At this game, which in our house is known as the "the night we almost got divorced" game, my husband was the home plate ump for a 14-and-under softball game which decided which team won a bid to go to Nationals. At this game, where he ejected me (in case you didn't read that part), I stopped by the field to bring him an extra drink. I stood near the bleachers that were next to the first base line. There were already two outs in the inning, and I felt some tension from the crowd sitting in those bleachers. After the batter took the first pitch, the ump let out a loud "Strike". Then I heard a father in the bleachers scream,

"Are you blind? Are you an idiot? That was clearly a ball."

I now recognized the source of the tension. Yes, this game had an irate parent. It's sad but it's a fact of organized sports that each team has one of those parents who cannot keep his or her mouth shut. These parents feel it is their right to try and sway, through intimidation, the way an umpire calls a game. My daughter played travel ball and varsity softball throughout high school. On each team, we had our share of parents who thought their kids were the next Babe Ruth. Okay, in our case, they were the next Babe Ruth with breasts. They believed their kids were the best, and this perception gave them the right to insult coaches, parents and umpires.

Back to this game – you know the one where my husband ejected me – Did I mention that already? I knew I should have left when I realized that there was a troublemaker parent in the vicinity, but like a good train wreck, I had to stick around and watch. The irate dad was standing on the bleachers, and he was clearly agitated. He was upset at everything from the balls and strikes calls to how the third base coach was telling his base runners to lead. He complained loudly, and he was so sure that the rest of the parents agreed with him. The other parents did not say anything to the irate dad. They chose to ignore him. After the second pitch, my husband called another strike. The irate parent ridiculed the ump again. My husband still ignored him. He is very cool behind the plate, but I could see his patience was wearing thin. Finally, the batter swung and missed the last pitch which ended the inning.

Well, it ended the inning for everyone but the father of the kid who struck out. He continued to scream. Even the other parents started to shift away from him. My husband watched for a second, and told the coach that if the dad did not calm down, he would be ejecting him. The coach kept apologizing for the father's actions, and then he told the dad to sit down and be quiet. Do you believe the parent did not listen to the coach? Instead, he started to curse – at my husband.

That's when I sort of got involved. I told him that he was an embarrassment and that this game was supposed to teach kids about sportsmanship and responsibility and teamwork. Now, the coach and the other parents got involved. They were yelling at this dad, and I was yelling at this dad, and he was yelling at me, and then my husband came over and glared at me and the dad, and he ejected us both. At that moment, I was a bit ticked off at the ump, but I realized that I did not help the situation at all. However, I think the crowd was happy I came because I gave the ump a good excuse to get rid of the parent from hell.

When my husband got home that night, I still was a little miffed. I couldn't let him think he could throw me out of places without paying a price for it. He apologized, but he said I left him no choice. "I probably would have ejected that guy in the next inning anyway," he confessed. "I give parents a little time to think. It's best for the kids if they don't see their parents ejected, but sometimes I have to take that step." I forgave him, and then the ump thought we were back to normal, so he tried to circle the bases at home with me. Silly, silly ump. It was my turn to eject him from the playing field.

The Near Electrocution of the Cable Guy

In an attempt to lower my phone bill, I signed up for the Triple Play from my cable company. What this means is that the cable company now has possession of my technology soul. They bill me for my phone, internet and TV.

Converting to the cable phone service did not come without glitches. The installation process which they promised would be painless resulted in the near electrocution of Cable Company's technician. He was drilling into the wall of my house when his drill hit the main power feed. Yes, you would have thought they would have trained him how not to electrocute himself, but apparently, he cut classes the day they were teaching this valuable lesson.

Luckily, my husband was home for the installation and pulled him away from the power before it was too late. There was smoke, a flash of light and the smell of burning rubber and then a very shaky cable guy. I started to call 911, but the technician said that he was fine and just needed to lie down. For two hours, he lay on my sofa with a cold compress on his head. I made him a ham and cheese sandwich for lunch and gave him my favorite PMS cookies for dessert -- Pepperidge Farm Milanos. I figured his hormones were probably in worse shape than mine since 200 volts of electricity had just coursed through his body.

I don't mean to sound uncaring, but his near death experience caused a few problems for me as well. The electrical surge blew out my power which required the services of an emergency electrician who had to repair the damage before the cable company could dispatch another technician to install the new phone system. So, I had no power, no computer, no phone and a traumatized cable man who was making himself at home and now calling me Donna. I guess he thought we bonded.

Eventually, everything was repaired, and the power was restored. The new technician put in the long awaited phone system, and we were on our way to enjoying our Triple Play features. When the service was up and running, the wounded technician decided to leave as well. Since the hour was so late, I did invite him to stay for dinner since we were now on a first name basis, but he had to get back to work and check in with his supervisor.

Do you know that I never heard from that cable guy again? I thought he would have called to say he was feeling better or to thank us for our caring hospitality, or for eating my favorite depression-lifting cookies or for saving his freaking life, but nothing. I thought he would have told his supervisor that we were nice to him, and they would have given us a free month of cable service as a reward. Okay, that was a hefty fantasy, but that's me, I dare to dream.

Anyway, the near electrocution incident soon became a distant memory. I repainted the back porch wall where his burnt skin left scorch marks. The cable service has worked almost exactly as I hoped. I embraced all the features–until I tried to leave a message for my dogs. Yes, I am one of those people who will call and leave a message for my dogs when I am away. I work from my house, so they are used to having a stay-at-home mom.

I was at the beach with my husband. I took out my cell phone to call the house so they could hear my voice. I heard my voice message and when I heard the beep, I started to speak. "Hi Girls. It's Mommy. I miss you and I will be home soon."

My husband gave me what I would describe as a quizzical look and asked, "What the hell are you doing?"

"Leaving the girls a message."

"We have Comcast. The dogs don't hear the message. The phone rings and goes to voicemail."

And just like that the light bulb went on in my head. For months, I have been leaving messages for the dogs – messages they could not hear. They could not retrieve my messages unless, of course, they know my access code and can push the buttons on the phone.

So, with this new revelation that my dogs are all alone without my voice to comfort them, I told my husband that I was not sure if I wanted to keep the cable phone service.

"You want to switch because the dogs can't hear your messages?"

When he said those words aloud, I realized how ridiculous the idea was. Honestly, the dogs seem to have adapted nicely to no messages. They do not look as if they have suffered at all. They are quite independent. Is it possible they don't need me anymore? I think I need a new puppy.

My New Life as a Lawn Mower Racing Champion

Each spring I take out my lawn mower and assess its condition. Well, what that means is I turn it upside down and remove the accumulation of gunk that I never removed from the blades the year before. It's true I am not a mower mechanic, but I do pick up on potential problems that might interfere with me maintaining my lawn mowing schedule. The one thing I did notice is that I need new wheels. I know this because by the end of last season, the self-propulsion feature on my mower had died. And I know *this* because I was huffing and puffing as I tried to push that stupid machine up the hill in my backyard.

I was going to ask for new wheels for my birthday, but by the time that comes around the mowing season would be at its peak, so I decided to give in and order them online. As I was looking for my wheels, I started to scout out the riding mowers that were for sale. Yes, this was a dare-to-dream moment, but even if I could afford one this year, I wouldn't get it. To me, a riding mower is the ultimate admission that I am getting old. I have a half-acre of land. I think I should be able to push a mower once a week across that vast expanse.

I admit that I get a twinge of jealousy when I see my neighbors riding around on their mowers having a grand old time. They are listening to music and singing, and they love to make fun of me for pushing my machine. But I just smile and keep quiet until I know they can't hear me over their super duper motors and then I scream,

"You are old and fat! Get off your keester and get some exercise!"

I know this is not a mature attitude, but it's the best I can do. Anyway, as I was reading about the mowers, I saw an ad on the page for lawn mower races. Yes, now driving riding mowers has become an official sport. There are rules as well as national and local chapters and specific races – it's legit. Founded in 1992, the United States Lawn Mower Racing Association (www.letsmow.com) wants people to celebrate the fun of lawn mowers. Contestants don't race for money, but they do get trophies. I initially thought the races were about who can cut a plot of grass the fastest, but I was mistaken. The mowers, which can get to speeds of 50 MPH, compete in races on tracks and fields, and these races are held at charity events, fairs, and car shows.

There are rules to the races too. Long-sleeved clothing and long pants must be worn as well as association-approved helmets. The most important rule--I think it's the most important rule because it is in all caps on the website--is that all cutting blades must be removed from the mower before racing. Personally, I think that is a good idea. Nothing brings down a good race like decapitating one's opponent or severing someone else's limb with a blade which has gone amok.

As I delved deeper into this organization, I started to think that I might like to do these races. Hey, it's sort of like extreme sports without all the flipping in mid-air requirements, and I always wanted a motorcycle but due to a lack of balancing skills, I never got to achieve that dream.

And to be honest, I don't think NASCAR wants me so maybe the Lawn Mowers Racing Association does. It would be a blast. I think I might do well at the sport. I have it on good authority – mainly Pennsylvania State Troopers, that I am quite capable of reaching and exceeding 50 MPH in any vehicle.

I think this sport could catch on. Hey, it could be the next soccer in the US, only more popular, and it could take over our sporting world. ESPN or CBS Sports can cover it too. They might need a new sport since, as of now, the NFL has not reached an agreement yet for the upcoming season. Maybe if the owners and players see how popular lawn mower races become, they might get nervous and reach an agreement sooner. And if they don't, we can all become lawn mower race fans. I think I might have to attend an event and see what this is all about. Today, I might be a mere spectator, but tomorrow a champion racer. How cool would that be?

The Mom Dance

One day, while I was visiting at my daughter's college apartment, she and her roommate were telling me how they took their other roommate's mom out to the bars for some dancing and college decadence. I was laughing along with the girls up until my daughter started to describe how this woman danced in the clubs. She called it the "Mom Dance".

I was a bit taken aback and asked, "What the hell is the Mom Dance?" At that point, the two girls stood up and started to sway in place at a brisk speed. Then they swung their arms back and forth simultaneously snapping their fingers.

Insulted by this little demonstration, I said, "Who dances like that? I don't dance that way!"

"Uh, yes you do. All moms do."

So, in an attempt to prove them wrong, I started to dance. And then it hit me! I do dance the Mom Dance. I never did before. I never had these lame moves. I was voted best dancer in grammar school. I danced on my fair share of tables in college (it was college – that's all I can say), and now I do the Mom Dance. My God, what is next - support hose?

The two girls saw my shock and tried to comfort me the best way they knew how.

"All moms dance the same way. It happens when you get old," said my daughter who was not a psychology major.

"It's okay, Mama Cav, my mom can't dance anymore either," said her roommate, the compassionate nursing major.

Need I say I was crushed? I have always felt youthful, and now my daughter and her entire generation were lumping me with the frumps who could no longer hold their own on the dance floor. When I got home, I began Facebooking my high school and college friends querying them about the Mom Dance. To my surprise, several had heard about our changing dance moves. The other two, who had not heard about the Mom Dance, left our chat to check their dance moves in a mirror. I tried to warn them that this was not a good idea, but their curiosity was too strong. The shock did prove to be too much as one came back with a box of chocolate doughnuts, and the other a bottle of Tequila which left her totally incapable of typing a coherent sentence. The rest of us finally convinced her to shut down the computer and go to bed.

Well, this whole Mom Dance thing got me thinking. If my once admired dance talent had morphed into something called the Mom Dance, what else in my life had morphed? What other transformations are waiting to take over my once youthful existence? I posed these questions to my daughter the next time she called, and she was ready and willing to give me the answers. (It's these tender mother-daughter moments that make me appreciate those species that are smart enough to eat their young.) Anyway, this is the list of "Mom Things" that the younger generation has noticed. I just want to say here and now that I do not remember these "Mom Things" with my own mother. Either that woman was an alien or she had me brainwashed, and if I was brainwashed, why the hell didn't she teach me how to do the same thing to my kid?

Mom Jeans – Apparently, it does not matter how thin or thick a mom is, she eventually seeks out jeans that sit comfortably upon the waist. Yes, Mom Jeans are meant for comfort, not style, and as my daughter pointed out "Mom jeans are a must because who wants to see their mom's thong hanging out the top of low rise jeans.

Okay, I had to give her credit on this one. I know very few women over the age of 35 who reach for a thong in the morning. It just doesn't seem like the natural thing to do.

Mom Undergarments – This goes along with the thong thing. According to my daughter, women go from wearing a thong to granny panties the instant a baby is born. Yes, apparently a baby brings with it from the birth canal a woman's first pair of old lady panties. Okay, it's true that we all own a pair or two of granny panties, but we don them when we are cleaning or mowing the lawn– doing things where we don't want to waste our good underwear.

I guess while we are on this topic – sucking-in underwear garments should be added to this list - Spanx® and another brand that some chick sells on a Sunday morning infomercial. She promises that her comfortable undergarments will eliminate love handles and muffin tops completely. Now, I was with a friend who bought these wonder products and tried them on. I almost had to call 911 to get her breathing again. So, under no circumstances will I join the other moms in their purchase of these items.

Mom Heels – okay, we all own that sexy pair of pumps or sandals with the four-inch heels. You bought them on sale at Bloomies or some other expensive store because they looked so sophisticated, and you swore you were going to wear them at least once a year. Alas, those heels have made it out of their box once, five years ago, for your cousin's wedding. You wore them for the ceremony, but you knew you were not going to last in them. So, before the reception, you went to the closest Payless store and bought a pair of comfortable flats so you could get on that dance floor and dance what you did not know at that time was the Mom Dance!

Mom Glasses – I can honestly say that I do not need Mom glasses or what are commonly known as reading glasses. I read fine. I can't see far, but who the hell cares about that? I go out to lunch with my friends and they all whip out these multi-colored, fashionable reading glasses that they bought in CVS at the display by the canes and walkers. And they all say the same thing when they put them on, "I hate that I need these glasses, but I don't mind because these are so cute."

Apparently, denial becomes our best friend too as we age. In any event, the one consolation I can take from learning about the Mom Things is that one day my daughter will have her own child, and I will be there with a pair of granny panties, flat shoes and a live band so she can do her first "Mom Dance" the second the kid hits the delivery room.

Is That Burning Hair I Smell?

I was having lunch with a friend, and she brought up the topic of her laser hair removal treatments. Now, immediately I became interested as this is the second time in about two weeks the topic has come up. The first time I discussed hair removal was with a friend of mine on Twitter. We were talking about getting revenge on whoever the "schmuck of the week" was in our lives, and I said,

"I can't beat him up because that would mean I would have to go to jail, and they don't let you shave your legs in prison, and I couldn't cope with that."

To which she responded,

"Get laser treatments first and then you do not have to worry about it!"

Now, let me emphasize that getting laser treatments did not make the difference between me doing bodily harm to someone or not; I don't think so anyway. To be honest, the guy was an idiot on a major scale, so he did deserve some kind of comeuppance. Anyway, the Twitter convo resulted in me getting a lot – and I mean a lot – of direct messages from men who wanted to weigh in on the whole hair removal topic.

This is how I break down the messages: 39 percent of the men thought no hair on women was extremely sexy; 52 percent said they didn't mind some hair on women, and a weird 9 percent of men liked very hairy women which made me wonder if they had a "Bigfoot" fetish thing going on.

Are these numbers accurate? Absolutely not. I don't do statistics. In fact, I only got a C+ in statistics in college and that is because I work-studied for the professors who taught statistics and logic. They were office mates and best friends and at the end of the semester when I took statistics, the one professor said to me,

"I am giving you a 'C' because you brightened up our dull office, but the 'C' is predicated on the fact that you never do statistics in any professional capacity." Now, most people would be insulted by this, but me, I saw an opportunity. So, I said in my best negotiation voice,

"Give me a C+, and I promise your office mate that I will never practice logic either."

"Done!" they both said quickly.

I probably should have shot for the 'B' but to be honest, it was not deserved. However, I am proud to say that I have kept my word. The science of Statistics and the art of Logic are nowhere to be found in my daily life.

I have digressed. Back to the lasers. My Twitter friend said she went for about six treatments, eight weeks apart, to remove leg, underarm and bikini-area hair. At the end of the scheduled treatments she was hair free – *everywhere!* So, my mind started to think if this was a good option for me. I have to admit that shaving is a pain figuratively while waxing is a pain literally. So, laser hair removal became one of those subjects that I stuck into my mental notebook with the promise that I would investigate later on.

So, a few days later, I was at the Macaroni Grill scarfing down my whole wheat vegetable pasta medley when my friend started to talk about her laser treatments that she was getting at her OB/GYN's office. I decided to be bold and ask for details.

"Do you have gray hair?" my friend asked.

"No, I haven't gone gray yet," I responded showing her the roots on my head."

"Not there!" she snapped back.

It took a moment, but then the light bulb turned on.

"Oh...*oh!* Down there? I didn't know it went gray. I must have missed the lecture on the changing colors of pubic hair in my catholic school health class. Well, no then."

"Well, you are still a good candidate."

Go figure. She explained that laser treatments, which are FDA-approved, need to be done before hair turns gray because lasers cannot remove light-colored hair. I looked that up and it is true. It seems lasers work ideally on light skin and dark hair.

My next question had to do with pain or the lack of pain. My friend said it feels a little like gentle rubber bands hitting your skin. She said, it sounds worse than it is, but there is a burning smell sometimes, so she had to keep checking to make sure that her vagina had not caught fire. I swear those were her words, and when she uttered them, the image that popped into my brain made me cough up my bowtie pastas. Now, if you think this conversation was entertaining to me, you would have laughed to see how it affected the two men dressed in suits sitting next to us.

It took every bit of control I had in me not to turn to them and say, "What, you never heard of vaginas on fire before?"

In all fairness to the eavesdropping men, they might have been listening for tips as well. It seems that more men are embracing the idea of body hair removal. While eyebrows, necks and chest hair have been traditional popular areas for waxing, electrolysis and now lasers, some men are looking into reducing the amount of hair at their bikini line. Men don't like to use the term bikini line, so let's just say the area where their crown jewels reside.

My last question had to do with the costs. It seems that insurance doesn't cover laser hair removal. That is a shame because I would jump at the opportunity if it did. But most treatments run about $200 or so, and I just can't justify that price tag. So, for now, the super silky razor or the torture of waxing is a more affordable alternative for me. However, if there are any laser experts who want someone to write a review on the treatments, drop me a line. I am always open for negotiation as long as you can assure me that my vagina will not burst into flames.

Old Friends and New Boobs

I had this freckle. Now, I am a fair-skinned person, so I have a ton of freckles, but this one was different. I would never have known it was different if a friend of mine had not noticed it at the beach one day. It was raised, but a few days earlier a bee stung me there, so I knew in my head that the new look to the freckle was more about the bee bite than something more sinister.

Still, my friend started to go on and on about all the things it could be until she made me crazy, so I called the dermatologist and had the damn thing removed. It turned out fine. The doctor looked at it and said, "It's a freckle with a bee bite, but since you're here, let's lob it off."

Anyway, as she was burning the freckle off my skin, she started to talk to me about other cosmetic procedures that she and her plastic surgeon partner do. She said, "You have a baby face, but sooner or later that baby face will show its age."

So, she sent me home with a few dozen brochures that showed me how I could look better. I am probably the most easily influenced person on the planet. I poured over those brochures lamenting the fact that I could not afford to do any of them right now. Not helping to assuage my "getting old" fears were my friends who offered a variety of comments such as "Wow, they can contour your chubby cheeks!" Or "What would you do if you didn't have that fat face?" Or "Why don't you just get your hair straightened instead with that Brazilian smoothing system?"

Well, at that point, I was not thinking my hair was an issue, but now I knew it was. My husband dismissed the doctor's comments with what I think was a sweet gesture. He said "I love that fat face. I married it, didn't I?" When my daughter called home, I told her about my freckle removal visit and the convo I had with my friends. Finally, someone who appreciated my "assets".

"Dad and I count on your hair especially when we are in crowds. We can spot you a mile away!" Then she went on to explain how when I would chaperone school trips, the kids wanted to be with me not because they loved my chaperoning skills but because they knew they would never get lost. Apparently, the consensus was that my hair was like a beacon of light guiding the little lost lamb home.

Who knew? Anyway, I did laugh off the whole cosmetic surgery thing within a few days, but about two weeks later, I met with some other friends for a girls' night out. I told them about my freckle experience, and they all easily admitted to having work done. One, had her boobs done and her tummy tucked; another friend had liposuction on her thighs, and the third, her eyelids lifted.

They were all so proud of the work, and to be honest, their doctors did a great job. The boob friend, whose new husband bought her "the girls" as a wedding gift, invited me to touch them, so I copped a feel to see what they were like, and I have to tell you I was impressed and a little jealous. I go to the gym at least three times a week, and I still have some problem areas. I even do that exercise to tone my chin and slim down my face – you know the one where you open your mouth really wide and then close it into a pucker. I do 10 reps of 10 per day. I usually do it while driving because it scares other drivers on the road. They think there is something wrong with me, and they leave me alone and let me go wherever I want.

Am I jealous that my friends got all this work done? No. Personally, I do like making improvements by exercising. Will there be a time when they start to look 20-something again, and I will be the really old friend they take pity on? If that happens, I might have to find older friends, but unfortunately, that takes a lot of effort.

I kicked myself for the feelings of self-pity that crept into my psyche, and I decided not to get caught up in this trap. I don't have anything against plastic surgery if it makes people feel good about themselves. But, it's not right for me -- now anyway. If I want to look perkier or flatter or thinner or whatever, I can still scour the Victoria's Secret catalogs and find an accessory item that will do the trick. As long as there is a push up bra, and tummy flattening underwear, I guess I can make do. The hair – well, the world will have to deal.

The Psychic and the Internet Minister

I went with my friend to the psychic. Yes, the psychic. I know so many of you have opinions on psychics, but can you just try to hold them in while I tell this story? The psychic is at a nearby tavern, so my friend and I use the card readings as an excuse to meet, have a few laughs, catch up on our lives and find out what our futures hold. I was seeking career advice and she needed guidance on her romantic life. As we were waiting for our individual turns, we started to talk about marriage or rather the idea of getting married again.

It is funny, that we both said, "Probably not" on our willingness to walk down the aisle for a second time but for very different reasons. She had been through a bad marriage and divorce and is happy with her life now. She likes having a special someone in her life, but she also likes the independence that comes with being single. Me, I am used to being married. I am lucky that I have been happily married for a long time, but let's face facts. To be married for a long time requires a lot of work. I'm not sure that I could find the same kind of connection that I have with my husband with another person, so I decided I would date but not marry.

We were patting ourselves on the back for being independent-thinking women when she got called back to see the psychic first. Fifteen minutes later, she runs back to the table with startling news: she is getting married to the guy she is dating!

After a few squeals of "Really, how exciting!" and "I knew you were meant to be!" and "What kind of dress do you want?" we calmed down and I said

"Hey, what happened to not needing a piece of paper to be happy?' "

"I don't need the paper, but I love him a lot, so why not take the plunge?"

I have to admit I was really happy seeing her so happy. So, then we started to talk about her wedding and what it would be like. She is a practicing Catholic but divorced, and well that means unless she is willing to pay $3000 or more for an annulment, no Catholic ceremony is waiting for her. However, I jokingly reminded her that there was nothing to worry about because as it turns out, I am an officially ordained minister thanks to a church on the internet.

Yes, I am a woman of the cloth. Okay, I admit I did it as a rebellious lark against my Catholic upbringing and to be honest, it was rather easy to do. I found an internet church that seemed to reflect my attitude on life. Its credo was "Always look to do good and never do harm to anyone or anything in the universe", and I thought that was nice. I try not to harm anyone. I did email them to ask if their philosophy included spiders in my house because, honestly, I feel strongly that they have to die. I am waiting on that response. All in all, this church's views were a new age version of the golden rule, so I knew I could live with that.

Next, they sent me material that I had to read. After I completing the course, I checked a few boxes, took a test, and a few minutes later, I got this wonderful email that said, "Congratulations Reverend Cavanagh!"

I could not help but emit a loud chuckle when I saw my new title.

Anyway, as my friend and I were sitting in the bar talking about her upcoming nuptials, she looked at me and exclaimed,

"You can marry us!"

"What? Oh, no! NO! NO! " The panic in my voice was evident.

"Yes, it's perfect. You can marry us! How great would that be?" she repeated.

"You want me to speak in public? I don't speak in public. That's why I write. You want me to officiate your wedding? I didn't even buy my minister kit yet. I don't even have a robe. I think I need a robe!"

"You have your daughter's Penn State graduation robe! That will work, and it's blue. You look good in blue."

It's true; I do look good in blue. I was starting to get excited about the prospect of doing this wedding thing especially if she arranged it in the Bahamas or someplace like that. The internet church people told me it was legal to perform weddings and officiate at funerals, but I never really thought about it. But what the hell - I guess I should say heck now, huh? Damn! Do I have to give up swearing? goddammit! I mean - oops! Anyway, I made a mental note to go online this week and buy my official wedding kit – just in case.

The Cleaning Lady Diaries

Friday is cleaning day for me. Yes, that is the day I ditch my computer and bring out my mop and bucket. I hate cleaning. Some of my friends view cleaning as some kind of Zen experience. I view it as torture. I used to have Janine clean my house twice a month. I got her through a friend, and my friend said that Janine was willing to take me on even though her client list was filled. I felt special. I was so excited about this domestic find that I vowed to make her time in my house as painless as possible.

The night before she was scheduled to clean, I would wipe down the sinks, shower and bathtub. I would move all the junk off my dressers, and make sure no shoes or clothes were left on any of the bedroom floors. I didn't want her to think she was working for a pig. My twisted brain surmised that if my house was too dirty, the cleaning lady would not want to clean it.

When Janine agreed to take me on as a client, she assigned me the Tuesdays, 8:30 AM cleaning slot. At first, she was a dream. She arrived and went to work; my house sparkled. The woman was Mary Poppins with tattoos and a smoker's cough. But then Janine's habits changed. She spent the first half hour drinking coffee at my kitchen table and telling me about her dysfunctional life. Then she would clean. About four months into her employment with me, she started not to show up at the scheduled time. Instead of showing up at 8:30, she would show up at 10:30, and some Tuesdays she wouldn't show up until Wednesday which left me frustrated because I could not plan my work schedule. So, I took a proactive approach and decided to talk to her.

"Janine, you know how much I love your work here," I stammered badly. "But I work from home, and…and I have to do phone interviews and…and write in my office upstairs and…and I try to have a professional atmosphere. I need to be able to plan my schedule, and when you don't show up on time or show up on another day, you…well, you sort of screw that schedule up. "

"What are you saying? Are you saying I get in the way of your writing or whatever the hell you do upstairs… like it's a real job? You think your work is more important than mine?"

Oops, this was not going well and in my mind, panic started to set in and I heard my mind screaming,

"Mayday! Mayday! Someone help, I am going down!"

But there was no rescue in sight. Janine shrugged her shoulders and made it clear she was not happy with my insistence that my time slot remain my time slot. However, Janine was a professional, and I hoped that she would honor my request.

Janine did not honor my request. In fact, she made it a point to never show up at my assigned time slot again. Finally, fed up, I made the drastic step to have my husband fire her. I know; I know. I am a coward, and I should have done the dirty work myself, but I had more interaction with Janine than he did. I was the one who was home when Janine came to clean. I became her sounding board for everything that was wrong with her life, and there was so much wrong. I heard all about her bad childhood, her yeast infections, her husband's erectile dysfunction, her brother's kleptomania (which I prayed was not a genetic condition) and her teenage daughter's stints in rehab.

If I fired someone with all that negativity going on, that negativity might vibrate back to me. Since my husband is not as big a believer as me in the power of positive and negative vibrations and what they can do to one's aura, he was the better choice to wield the axe.

The firing did not go well, and my friends who used Janine's cleaning services were annoyed with me too. I guess Janine viewed my friends as traitors since they referred her to me. She started to slack off and began not showing up at their appointed time slots.

In order to make amends to both Janine and my pissed off friends, I found my ex-cleaning lady another gig. Yes, I looked high and low until I filled my former assigned cleaning time slot.

With Janine fully employed, I relaxed into my own self-cleaning schedule. How has this worked out? Well, I am not the best domestic diva. I can clean, but it's not something I long to do. Will I get another cleaning woman in the future? Probably not. I can't take the pressure that having a cleaning woman entails. I was always trying to please her. Now, that I have made peace with my sloppiness and the dust bunnies under the beds, life is good again.

Made in the USA
Charleston, SC
28 May 2016